Happ,

Priscilla Giesbrecht

September 14, 2013

From your Friends
Eddie & Gerry Schneider

Dear Priscilla
From

Mr. and Mrs. Edward Schneider
3030 Duhart Church Rd
Stapleton, GA 30823-7186

CHANGED

An Apocalyptic Story with Hope and a Solution

BILL WESENBERG

iUniverse, Inc.
Bloomington

Changed
An Apocalyptic Story with Hope and a Solution

iUniverse books may be ordered through booksellers or by contacting:

iUniverse
1663 Liberty Drive
Bloomington, IN 47403
www.iuniverse.com
1-800-Authors (1-800-288-4677)

ISBN: 978-1-4759-7179-8 (sc)
ISBN: 978-1-4759-7180-4 (hc)
ISBN: 978-1-4759-7181-1 (e)

Library of Congress Control Number: 2013900788

Printed in the United States of America

iUniverse rev. date:1/25/2013

CONTENTS

ACKNOWLEDGMENTS

Most of this book was written while I was sitting in my recliner chair in our living room. It is not my own. As the sprit of God brought these thoughts to my mind, I wrote them down on paper. Therefore, it is my belief that all the thanks should go to Him. For one to realize the humble servant's attitude, Christians must not take credit for ourselves but truly believe. I have nothing that I have not received from God. Therefore, if you can gain anything from this book, give all praises to God, our Father, and Jesus, His Son, and the Holy Spirit, whose work is on this earth.

Thanks also to iUniverse and everyone who helped with the making of this book. And of course, many thanks go to you readers.

AUTHOR NOTE

The author recommends reading this book all the way through. Then if you have questions or you are curious and want to know more, look up all the scriptures for any or all chapters to see for yourself if the Bible agrees with the message of this book.

The Puzzle of Life

Life is a puzzle with pieces
We all must navigate through.
Many shapes, and sizes, and colors,
Experiences for us to pursue.

A beautiful picture on the box
Made it seem all would be grand.
A nice big man and a little boy,
A scene for all ages to stand.

Inside the box was a paper,
Instructions for completion, you see.
It said some pieces were missing.
To complete, it would take more than me.

I started the puzzle with joy.
It seemed very easy at first.
The borders just whipped along.
I thought, *It'll be little time at worst.*

Inside, the puzzle was harder.
Time seemed to slow all the more.
I became weary, drowsy, and tired.
Another day, I'd work on the core.

It was discouraging, to know
Not all of the pieces were there.
To finish, would take someone else
And likely, even a prayer.

One day, I sat down to finish.
I used all the pieces I had.
The picture was gorgeous, except
In the middle, it looked very bad.

Wondering what to do next,
The man in the picture came by.
He gave me a little tip.
He said, "I'll tell you why

The pieces in the middle
Cost all you have to obtain.
To get them, you must be humble
And call on the Savior's name.

Jesus longs to complete the picture.
He'll be the nice big man.
You can be the little boy.
He'll bring you to heaven's land.

So don't give up on the puzzle.
Continue to listen to Him.
His voice is soft and lowly.
His light is bright, not dim."

Life's middle belongs to Jesus.
Never let yourself forget
If you want to be in heaven,
He must finish the picture yet.

—Bill Wesenberg

Introduction

This book describes many events from the King James Version of the Bible. Some experiences are fictionalized, but these are included for the purpose of helping us understand the great beyond. It is certain that some of the ideas expressed here may not actually happen. It is humanly not possible to comprehend eternity. We can take our minds only so far before they reach their limit, and understanding beyond that point ceases. God wants to talk to each of us, and if we let Him, He will reveal enough understanding to us so that we can walk the streets of gold someday!

This text is about you and me ... or people named "you" and "me." We are experiencing our last days on earth and the beginning of hell. Our experience is from a different perspective than people normally consider. The earth becomes the fire source, and space is the bottomless pit. You and I go through terrible stress as we see your mother and others rise to heaven. These rising souls appear as bright flashes all around us. We are speechless and terrified.

At our judgment, we hear the terrible words: "Depart from me, I never knew you." Hell begins, and we are put into the bottomless pit of space because of our beliefs and how sinful we have been. Hell brings terrible physical suffering. Brimstone clouds are the worst part. Black fire torments us beyond speakable words. Then we come to know something much worse as love is withdrawn and nobody cares about us. God is not here. Jesus has gone back to heaven, and we are left without hope in darkness forever.

We wonder how others here in hell are faring, so we decide to interview our peers. We hear why they came here and what they think now that they have experienced hell. We find that everyone is repentant. All are blaming themselves, and everybody here wishes they could live their lives over again. We hear that the devil and his angels suffer in the worst part of hell because they rose up against God and were cast out of heaven, doomed forever.

Then in a flash, we realize that our experience has been a dream, and we have a second chance. What will we do now? After this dream experience, we refuse to go to hell. We must find the way to heaven, so we go to the Bible, the roadmap to heaven. Whatever we must do, we will do to follow this roadmap. Making commitments, giving up our selfish desires, loving all others, giving God first place in our lives, and confessing our sins are all part of this "narrow way." We don't like humbling ourselves, but we will. We have to. We don't have an option.

Chapter 1 is about the end of time—the last day on earth. It will give us some idea of what may happen and how the judgment will come for both saved and unsaved. The revealing of the power of God will be awesome.

Chapter 2 will give us some ideas of how hell could happen, the devils being the first partakers—the earth burning to a hot flaming ball, love being withdrawn for the unsaved, complete darkness, and the start of suffering that will only become worse.

Chapter 3 is about terrible suffering, brimstone, and unquenchable fire—fire that it seems would kill us but doesn't and never will! It brings out thoughts of hopelessness and aloneness and a realization of pleasant things we'll miss forever. Panic and fear are constant, the 3-D picture revealed, and doom becomes real.

Chapter 4 will reveal some of that which will be in our minds. Our minds will be more alive at that point than they are now. The knowledge that we had a chance to go to heaven and forsook it will torment us forever. The presence of others brings no pleasure because love is over; nobody cares about us. Children are not here in hell! We can dwell on bad things only as nothing good remains.

Chapter 5 is a mirror for you. If you see yourself in a situation like those being interviewed, now is time for you to change and repent of your sins. If you can read this book, there is hope and opportunity for you to be saved. Sinners that do not repent will never be accepted in heaven, so check yourself and see if God has forgiven you through Jesus. If not, now is the time!

Chapter 6 brings us a very big surprise. We were doomed—hell and our suffering felt real. But we came out. It was a dream. We have another chance. Real hell will be much worse. So now we go to the Bible. We will study and find the way to heaven. By God's grace and our determination, we will never go to that terrible, everlasting hell. Back and forth, we discuss experiences from the Old Testament. We begin to get the picture of God's ways for mankind. We must make the commitment soon.

Chapter 7 introduces us to Jesus. He is the only one who can save us from our sins. His teachings seem to be different than our thinking. It sure comes across as a humble way while we read and consider some of His miracles and teachings. We also study His followers who tried to be like Him.

Chapter 8 is about our conversion experience. The whole world looks different. Hate and mistrust are gone. Love and peace is ours. Joy and forgiveness become a part of us. This surely is the contented life.

Chapter 9 brings us to the real Christian life and obedience. Jesus didn't expect to just save us, but He does expect that we should live for Him, follow His teachings, and listen closely to His Holy Spirit. When He ascended to heaven, He promised to send His Holy Sprit to guide us.

Chapter 10 is our reward for being faithful Christians. God will bring us back to Him. Though we don't fully understand the spirit world, we know heaven will be different and a much, much better place than Earth.

CHAPTER 1
THE LAST GREAT DAY

"HELLO, HELLO, IS ANYBODY home? Hello."

"Yes, I'm here."

"Why don't you come over today so that we can enjoy the day together."

"Okay, I'll be there in fifteen minutes."

"Hi and welcome to you."

Everything seems normal. The sun comes up. Birds sing. The sky is partly cloudy. The season is fall. A crispness is in the air. I look over to you and say, "What a great day to be alive. Let's do something special today."

And then it happens—a very loud noise, so loud we have never heard a noise like this before. It seems like many thunderclaps booming. We run to the window to see what is happening. Scared, uneasy, and beside myself, I view the sky rolling back like a scroll. At this moment, I know instantly what is happening. As all the past teachings cross my mind, it becomes very clear. *The end has come!*

A feeling of doom starts to come over me! My mind starts

to race oh-so-fast. *Am I ready for this day?* I ask myself. I never intended to be lost. Maybe God would be merciful, even though I did things as I wanted to. I glance over at you, and you look terrified. I must ask, "What's wrong?" You are speechless, and as words refuse to come out, I glance toward the window again. Celestial beings are coming out of the sky. I think I have just seen Jesus. *Is that God Himself way in the distance?* The face of Jesus looks very angry. Now I remember from my teachings how Jesus would come back to judge the earth. All the love and kindness, gentleness, and forbearance would cease. Judgment would be real and forever. Only those who repented of their sins and accepted His atonement and followed in obedience would be saved!

A supernatural power begins to move us outside. There seems no way to resist. Though I want to stay in, I can't. I begin to realize that I am losing control and that we don't have the power to make our own choices anymore! Finding ourselves out on the grass, looking up and around, we come to know many of the things the Bible said would happen.

Down the road at the cemetery, graves open up. People emerge, some shouting, many asking for rocks and mountains to fall on them, wanting to be covered back up instead of facing Jesus the judge. This is so surreal. *How can this be?* I think. All at once, I hear your voice. "Where are the sirens? Where are the police? Isn't anyone going to do something?"

I look up again, and for the first time, I notice that the sun has become dark and the moon is the color of blood—as the Bible said they would turn. Every once in a while, there seems to be a flash of bright light as someone ascends upward toward ... where? Heaven? Somehow, a multitude of people gathers together, multitudes and multitudes coming together for what? Their judgment? And then

I see her, your mother! She goes past us. She's ascending upward! Do you see how her face shines? Look how bright she is! Then with a terrible cry, I hear you say, "Mom, wait for me! Mom, please wait for me! I want to go with you! I can't stay here!"

Tears run like a fountain. Joy seems like it happened years in the past. All the while, your mother keeps ascending, and you come to realize that she is not coming back.

Heartache, crying, pain, and misery are all around, and yet a quiet, subdued seriousness has everyone spellbound, wondering what will come next. The realization that our bodies have changed has just became apparent. You remember the Bible said that in the twinkling of an eye, when the last trumpet would sound (remember that terrible thunder's blast?), we would be changed from corruptible to incorruptible and from mortal to immortal.

A young man appears. He is completely beside himself. He says that he and his brother had been sleeping in their beds when all at once, his brother was taken. An extreme force moved the brother through the house and out of the door, he says. As he ran to see what was happening, he caught a glimpse of his brother steadily advancing upward. He watched until he could see the brother no more. It was a very troubling experience for him.

Another woman approaches us. She and her friend had been grinding flour at the mill. As the great noise subsided, her friend also began rising! She tells us her friend was saying something about going to be with Jesus. She says a very happy look of rejoicing appeared across her friend's face. She's so upset that it seems nothing can comfort her.

As if these two experiences aren't enough, we behold with our own eyes two men working in a field nearby. One of them is making a terrible commotion. We look just in time to see the other man rising into the sky to be with Jesus in heaven. His body and face shine brightly like the sun. I can't help wondering why I am not rising up and what this means for me.

Jesus is arranging many books. The books contain all the deeds of the unforgiven—those who never repented of their sins. As the Great White Throne appears, the judge of all the earth prepares to sit upon His throne. A separation is underway and will continue as the Good Shepherd divides His sheep from His goats, with the saved (sheep) going to heaven and the lost (goats) going to hell.

As far as we can see, people are still gathering. They come from every tribe and nation. Those who ascend from the earth seem to be fewer and fewer. Way over yonder, a line is forming, and it looks like we'll have to take our turn meeting the judge. With a slim hope, there's a way out. Maybe God will grant me a place on the right-hand side. I encourage you to hold up and hope that somehow we'll make it through.

We wait for a long time; although, as you say," we don't know how long". The clocks have quit working. No one knows the time. It seems like days have come and gone, though darkness hasn't overtaken us yet. Our neighbor is trying to start his car, but to no avail. Some are trying to go back into their houses. However, their bodies won't let them. Though their minds scream to run and hide, their limbs simply can't move very much. Many are attempting to escape to somewhere. They find that nothing works. The Bible told us time would be no more. We just never fathomed what the end of time would really be like.

Listen! Can you hear what's being spoken? Did those people tell Jesus about all the good works they did? Are they trying to change His mind? It appears as if they believe they should be saved. If I hear right, Jesus is saying, "Depart from me. I never knew you."

Oh, what disappointment—going to the left-hand side and being forsaken forever to have no hope throughout eternity." Will you look at that crowd of people at the left side of Jesus?" So many are missing out on heaven. You remember the Bible said many would follow the broad road that leads to destruction. I have a sinking feeling about us. When will we take our turn? Isn't there a way out of this terrible day? Is the opportunity to be saved really past? How will we bear this terrible burden?

The earth seems to be heating up under my feet, and that brings back to mind the fact that the Bible said the earth will melt with fervent heat. I wonder if the process has already started from deep within the earth, and if so, what are we going to do?" What can we do?" It's almost our turn to face Him. The line seems to be going faster and faster. No one will be left out. The Bible reveals that everyone who ever lived would face judgment. The Bible also told us that everyone chooses when they will serve, and by the choices they made, they chose their destiny—that has me scared to face Him. I need another chance, but it's too late!

Some noises attract our attention over yonder by the horizon (straight away from Jesus), where a multitude of ugly beings weep and moan. They look very scared. They wring their hands, and it looks as if they are trying to protect the leader of their group. As we slowly catch on to who these beings are, hatred overcomes us. We see them as the foes of our souls, and we want to blame the devil for our presence down here. I say to you, "Let's do something about this." Bad feelings only make things worse as we realize we aren't going anywhere except where the great power of God is bringing us!

The devil and his angels are not in line to be judged. Their doom is already sealed. God pronounced judgment on them many years before. They have known how their end will be, and the only pleasure for them has been to take as many people away from God as they could. Oh, the temptations they troubled us with. Oh, the heartaches they caused. Oh, the wrong choices they helped us to make, though we knew better. Oh, the times we followed our fleshly desires as they tempted us with the easier road to take.

Now I say to you, "Here we are. It is almost our turn." Earthly life is over, and truly, it was like a vapor—very short indeed!

As the judging voice of Jesus calls my name, a dart shoots through me! A penetrating and piercing look by Him reveals my life! As my record is read, I begin to feel that there must be a terrible misunderstanding. My intentions were good. I wanted to be saved. I helped others when I could. I went to church most of the time. I was a good citizen. My neighbors thought well of me. I gave time and money to help others. I try to tell Jesus all these good things I did, but He looks at me and says, "I never knew you. You are not my child! I shed my blood for you, and you rejected me. You wasted my blood that could cover your sins. You are cursed. To the left-hand side you must go. You are cursed into the everlasting judgment of hellfire!"

Terror grips my heart! Mercy is no more! The love of Jesus, which flowed so freely, is over for those on the left-hand side. As I turn to the left, because there is no other way, I hear Jesus call your name! With a sense of hopelessness, helplessness, and numbness, I believe your trial will turn out much like mine. I truly feel sorry for you! The thought that we really had a chance to be saved and go to heaven and we forsook that chance is overwhelming me. I am beside myself. While I am feeling sorry for myself, I hear the words ring out to you: "I don't know you. You are not my child. You spurned my call. You rejected my invitation. Depart from me. You are cursed into everlasting punishment forever!"

Because of the finality of Jesus's words and because you know there is no other way, you walk over to me. At that instant, an uncontrollable crying overtakes both of us. People are crying and moaning everywhere. Men are still calling for the rocks and mountains to fall on them. The earth seems to be getting hotter under our feet. Peace and joy are forgotten. The most terrible part of this terrible experience is that we had a chance to be saved. The call had come. Jesus had invited us to be His children. He had made the way for whosoever would come to salvation. The blame for where we are rests solely on us!

It seems people have lost their direction. No one knows what to do next. Confusion is everywhere. All the while, the multitudes of people become larger and larger. Our friendship cools as we realize there is nothing we can offer each other. There seems to be no comfort for each other. We are more alone than ever before. Is there anything that could lift our spirits?

The answer to this question is no! As we glance over to the devil and his angels, we see they are suffering tremendously. A fire has broken out, and they are in it, tossing and turning, wailing and gnashing, moaning and groaning. The Bible said hell was created for the devil and his angels. It seems that reality bears this out—they will be the first partakers. It seems there would be some comfort to see the devils receive their just due. It is amazing that even though they led us astray, no comfort is felt. There isn't any comfort in realizing that all who are left behind are doomed, that their lot is the same as our lot, except for degrees of suffering. Hope is ended forever!

Though we didn't notice before, another scene comes into view. An angel with one foot on land and one foot on the sea declares that time would be no more. He stands there along with other angels; they seem to be keeping order by their presence and spirit, and it becomes clear that nothing will get by them. The all-seeing eyes of God will reveal everything. The Bible said every eye would see Him and no unrepentant, sinners would enter heaven. Some men are still calling for rocks and mountains to fall on them. It feels like all from the left-hand side are experiencing hopelessness and doom. We come to realize it's only a matter of moments before hell will swallow us up and punishment will be everlasting.

The judgment continues, although the line of people seems to be getting shorter. And then I say to you, "Do you hear that beautiful music? Look up." The angels and the saved ones are singing. It sounds so beautiful we almost forget our situation for a moment. We see Moses, Abraham, David, Daniel, and all the prophets of the Old Testament. Peter, James, John, Matthew, Mark, and Luke, the apostle Paul, and many of his fellow laborers are singing the song of the redeemed. Christians of all ages are praising God and waiting for Jesus to return to heaven after the judging of the earth is over. The martyrs who died for their faith are glowing even more than the other faithful ones. Then we see your mother and many others whom we know—family and friends who made the sacrifice to be true Christians. They are singing and praising God. They have a look of inexpressible joy on their faces! No one up there seems to be troubled about anything. Then you ask, "Can anyone imagine a life with no trouble, no heartache, no pain? It sure looks like they have attained indescribable blessedness in a blissful realm far beyond what we ever thought!"

The singing continues drifting down from above. Fearful voices bring us back to our surroundings, and we cannot be comforted. The singing, the glory, and the pureness of the saved only makes us more uncomfortable. The realization that we also had the chance to be in heaven and that we didn't take life very seriously is torment to our souls. Now it is easy to see what we should have done. Why, oh, why, couldn't we see before?

A group of people moves toward us. Their voices are hushed. If I hear correctly, it seems they think they have fooled God! It becomes apparent that they are the cremated ones. By having themselves burnt to ashes and scattered over land or sea, they believed God would never find them. How little they know of God's greatness and how in the resurrection we would all come forth to an immortal life and our souls would live on throughout eternity. Not even one soul who ever lived escapes the judgment of God. From the land or sea, from being eaten by beasts, or being encased in cement, or any other accident or disaster—all come forth to be judged and rewarded by their faithfulness or unfaithfulness.

Then it dawns on us. There aren't any children left behind. Each of them, every last one, has gone to heaven. They stand on the golden shore, saved—God hadn't called them. They are not accountable for their sins. The fairness of God wouldn't make them responsible until their understanding could comprehend the plan of Jesus and His salvation. Millions and millions of children are rejoicing up there. Jesus loved little children and said that unless we become like them, we would in no way enter the kingdom of heaven. Maybe that is where we went wrong. Instead of being humble, we were overtaken by pride and high-mindedness, thinking we knew everything and had figured the world all out. Here we are … lost, lost forever.

The judgment is almost over; the line of people is almost depleted. The earth is getting hotter. Great drops of sweat run over our bodies. The mood of the people deteriorates with every moment. We decide to check on the devil and his angels one more time. The sight is terrible. In the flames of torment, rolling and tossing, up and down, over and over, without mercy, without love, without any ray of hope, without any chance of improvement, they are suffering beyond imagination. There is no one to care, no one to help, no one to understand. If the devil could redo his big mistake, he surely would not have challenged God in heaven. By doing so, there was war in heaven, and the devil and his angels were cast out. His end was sealed. He never had another chance, and that is where we made such a big mistake, because we did have another chance. Though sin passed onto us, Jesus made a way. He gave us another chance, and we squandered that chance! How foolish!

The high and noble ones, the rich and popular, the rulers and wise ones—all are for the most part here! On the left-hand side, the humble hearts seem scarce. Most of them must have gone to heaven. The Bible told us, "Ye must be born again;"(John 3:3), meaning the old human way of doing must die and a "new life" in Christ must come forth. Those who truly repented of their sins and followed God's Spirit, those who obeyed the Bible and followed God's little voice, are not here. At least we haven't found any people like that. It must be they were those flashes of light ascending upward when the trumpet sounded.

At the end of the line of judgment stand those big Roman soldiers, the ones who crucified Jesus. They said way back then,

"Let His blood be on our hands. We and our children will take responsibility of crucifying Him."

They surely never thought they would meet Him again. Now the showdown of all showdowns is underway. All evil is being judged. These soldiers are quivering and shaking beyond anyone we have ever seen! They are so scared that their legs refuse to hold them up. As they fall and rise again and try not to look Him in the eye, the voice of Jesus penetrates their being.

"Though you drove the nails through my hands and feet, though you spit on me, though you put a crown of thorns on my head, though you parted my garments, though you treated me very cruelly, I would have forgiven you if you would have repented. You didn't and now your punishment will be greater than most. Though you slew me, you knew I arose again. You had a tremendous opportunity to accept me. To the left-hand side you must go!"

The mood of the people becomes even more hopeless. We know that things are only going to get worse, much worse! Jesus and the angels prepare to leave. The earth is getting hotter under our feet. Like Jesus did when He walked the dusty roads of Galilee, he only says what needs to be said. He has already given each one of us our eternal reward, so He has nothing more to say, and then ... He starts ascending. As He slowly rises from the earth with each of the heavenly angels going with Him, a terrible lonely feeling sweeps over our souls. An indescribable feeling like no other feeling we have ever had overtakes us. The idea of no love is beyond comprehension. The absence of hope is beyond reasoning. The thought of no escape from our situation is so terrible we cannot bear it.

We can hardly see them now. Jesus and the angels are almost out of sight. The Bible told us Jesus had the keys to hell, and now we know He is about to use them. Though we know it is too late, many are still crying out, "Can anyone help us?"

Scripture References for Chapter 1

1. Matthew 24:30
2. Matthew 24:31
3. 2 Corinthians 7:9-16
4. John 5:26–29
5. Revelation 6:12
6. 1 Corinthians 15:51–54
7. Matthew 25:32–33
8. Revelation 10:6
9. Matthew 7:13
10. 1 Peter 4:17–18
11. Matthew 25:41
12. Revelation 19:20
13. James 4:14
14. Matthew 7:22–23
15. Mark 8:38
16. Revelation 22:17
17. 1 Corinthians 15:19
18. Matthew 10:28–30
19. John 9:39–41
20. Revelation 15:3
21. Revelation 21:3–4
22. Luke 16:10–13
23. 1 Corinthians 14:20
24. Revelation 12:7–9
25. Romans 3:23
26. 1 Corinthians 1:26
27. John 3:5–7
28. Revelation 1:7
29. Matthew 27:28–35
30. Revelation 1:18
31. Revelation 6:14
32. 2 Timothy 4:1
33. Philippians 2:10–11
34. Revelation 6:16

35. 1 Thessalonians 4:16–17
36. Matthew 24:39–40
37. Revelation 20:11–12
38. Revelation 11:18
39. Matthew 7:21–23
40. 2 Peter 3:10
41. Matthew 7:21
42. Revelation 20:10
43. 2 Peter 2:9–10
44. Revelation 20:12
45. Matthew 25:41–46
46. Matthew 13:12
47. Matthew 24:12
48. Revelation 10:2–6
49. Revelation 1:7
50. 2 Thessalonians 1:8–9
51. Romans 12:1
52. John 5:29
53. Luke 18:16–17
54. Peter 5:5–6
55. Revelation 22:17
56. Romans 5:11–15
57. Acts 20:19
58. 1 Kings 19:10–14
59. Matthew 27:25
60. Luke 23:34

CHAPTER 2
THE BEGINNING OF HELL

A S JESUS REACHES HEAVEN, He turns toward earth and says, *"Let hell begin."*

Just as God had spoken into existence the world to begin, Jesus had the power to speak the beginning of hell! Many things start happening. The earth is becoming very hot. All people left behind begin to rise up above the earth's atmosphere. Each one takes his or her place where the great power of God causes him or her to be, beginning with the devil and his angels. They will be the closest to the earth. As the earth melts with fervent heat, each one will then have his or her place in hell by degrees, depending on how accountable we are.

Our place (yours and mine) is just a little above the devils, not because we were so bad but because we knew the call had come and we had been taught the right way. Because we rejected Jesus, we have a very undesirable place! As we rotate round and round the earth in the orbit God put us in, we begin to believe the Bible and the Word of God like never before.

Though we can see up in heaven and down to earth, it becomes apparent that as the Bible had said, there is a great gulf fixed so much so that no one can pass beyond it. I can tell by looking at you that you are trying to figure out how we can get out of this place. If we could all live our lives over again, we are sure everyone would accept God's plan, so we wouldn't be here—all would surely repent, forsaking their sins. Even though hell has hardly started, the suffering is already beyond anything earth gave us.

As we go round and round, we can see the earth below in great detail: our homes, our cars, our lands, the many things we had and places we could go, the great landmarks and monuments, the countries, oceans, states, lakes, trees, and animals. With each passing round, it seems the earth is getting hotter. Damage is evident. Animals are dying by the thousands. The trees and lands are withering. The water in the lakes is beginning to boil. We see houses on fire everywhere!

We are very hot. Our tongues are very dry, and I hear you crying for water. Just a little would do—if someone could please help, I know we would be very grateful. Sad to say, I don't expect that to happen! There isn't any water near us, and there's no one who can go to get some. So we suffer on. What else can we do! If we had the option to just die, that would be great. If this suffering would just end!

Looking down again as we pass my old homestead, a shocking scene comes into view. The fire is tremendous. Smoke bellows upward. The trees burn.

Every inch of the whole place is on fire. Even things that wouldn't burn before are burning now. The fire is so hot it looks like steel is melting. All life below—animals, plants, insects—all have perished. The fish, whales, sharks, and all sea life float on the rivers, lakes, and oceans. The boiling waters have cooked them, and it is a terrible mess!

Over to our right, we hear a man who must have had many earthly possessions. It is becoming clear to us that he has just spotted his place down below. As he witnesses the fire consuming his possessions, he starts to scream as loud as he possibly can. His face is completely red. You say to me, "I never saw a man so mad before."

An awful feeling comes upon me—to think that he would still be possessive of his earthly things. I wonder, *Doesn't he feel repentant now? Wouldn't he accept Jesus if he could have another chance? Did he believe after the judgment he would resume life as normal? Didn't he know that all of the earth and all therein would burn? Didn't someone tell him?* We hear him in the distance for a long time as we continue rotating around the earth.

As we look down, we see what used to be Europe. Europe was a great earthly kingdom. There was much to burn—many old buildings and monuments, many new skyscrapers, and modern things of every kind. Fire and smoke are rampant, burning everything. You are beside yourself as you view the unthinkable destruction, and you say to me, "This is unbelievable! This fire isn't just burning everything in its path. It is everywhere! We were told! We read about it! It was preached, but we didn't comprehend the reality of what we are seeing now. We never did."

We hear a raging voice, a blasphemous voice, a voice that makes us shudder to the very core of our being. I ask you who is talking. You respond, "I don't know, but he must have been a very wicked person."

Somehow, it becomes clear to us that he was responsible for killing many people, and because we are passing over Europe, we wonder, *Was that Hitler?* Frightening thoughts come to mind. It seems the past of all ages is being revealed to us. Some of the most unpleasant times of history are being revealed as we are partakers of the beginning of hell with the most ungodly of ungodly people of the past. I must ask the question again, *Why did we come here?*

The pain and thirst are ever with us. Tormenting thoughts of blaming ourselves are ever before us as we ponder our situation. The theme repeats over and over, "Had I only, had I only!" It is also troubling to know that hell hasn't been experienced in its completeness yet. It will become much worse.

We are moving on! The continent of Africa is coming below us, and we see a different picture. The fire is still here, although there aren't nearly as many of the great man-made things to burn. The cities have some. The countryside is dotted with small structures of earthen materials. Most of the people living here didn't have much, and their goals were different than we were used to seeing and feeling all around us. Their lifestyles were simple, and some may never have heard of the Christian way. Jesus knew them, but they had never heard of Jesus. God had a way of freeing Himself with all, and though we don't know how, God knew honest hearts. Some of these people went to heaven, and some with limited knowledge of Jesus are in the farthest outside orbits of hell. Their punishment will be less severe than those who knew or those who tried not to know. God made it so! God's knowledge knew how to make us responsible to accept Jesus and His way (the way of the cross). Oh, had we only done so!

We see the Holy Land, where Jesus walked, talked, and died for our sins. On the cruel cross, He gave Himself so we could be saved. By dying, He gave us the choice to be redeemed from sin.

Because sin would never enter heaven, again our choice should have been His way at all costs. If so, we wouldn't be here now! Many of Jesus's own people (the Jews) rejected Him. That He made this land his home means nothing now. The tomb, the city of His birth, the place of His death, the temples He taught in—all of these are burning now. Fire leaps up everywhere, and it is very clear that earth life means nothing now and will never mean anything again.

Seeing this destruction coming to the places we read about so often is sad. The sites of Bible stories that our mothers read to us while we were sitting on thier laps disappear in flames. How inspiring they were, especially the ones about Jesus and all the miracles He performed. Precious memories they are. It certainly is too bad we can't enjoy those experiences now! So foolish for us to enjoy the pleasures of sin for a season and now miss all the glories of heaven we could have enjoyed forever! Now I feel the need to ask you, "Do you think we can get some rest? My body is so tired. So much has happened. The pain is so great, the thirst so real. Is there some way this all could be just a dream? If we called on God now, do you think He would hear us? Are we really in a place without love and understanding? Are we really in a place without hope? Are all the doors shut?"

A very big and dark land appears. I must report that we don't receive any rest! No, instead we just keep going and seeing scenes we never imagined. The lands of Russia are vast and wide. Many people came from this land, and their history contains much harshness for the common person. So many people died by the hands of their leaders. Where are they now? We suppose some are here in hell and some repented and are in heaven. Surely, God will reward the darkness of the rulers with terrible suffering. Fire burns everything. The flames leap higher than we've seen so far.

Earthquakes are leveling mountains, and valleys are being filled. Everything is melting. As we pass by, we can feel the extra heat rising up to meet us. What will all of this look like the next time we come around?

China and India—so many people came out of these countries. Homes are everywhere. People's dwellings are burning. The fire has so much fuel and burns with fierceness beyond the others'. We can't help but wonder where all these people went. Then you ask if I realize how big hell is. Thinking for a moment of the space programs of the world and how far away many objects we knew of were, I understand. Hell is very, very big. I must wonder if God made it so that we may not see, feel, or know of others being there. Aloneness will be a punishment in itself. We see many gods of earthly materials being destroyed in these lands. Many of these people were very superstitious and worshipped strange gods. Now they are burning. Those who trusted in them are beside themselves as they realize how powerless their gods are and how foolish they were for trusting in the earthly gods of this world.

Once in a while, we still catch a glimpse of the devil and his angels. The flames of hell have reached them. All of the power he had while on earth is gone! His mission to get back at God for being cast out of heaven has failed. Because the devil's punishment is worse than any person's, it is very plain to see he hasn't any pleasure for causing people to sin. As always, he will not look us in the eye. His sneakiness gives him away just like his earthly temptations were always untrue. He was a liar from the beginning. His punishment is the very worst part of hell forever.

Passing over Indonesia and the little countries to the north and around Australia is another experience. The fire is burning all, so much so it appears as though even the water is on fire. Can it be, or does it just look that way from here because the land masses are close together? One thing is for sure: the ocean waters are boiling, and steam is rising. These possibilities never came to mind before, so it is with some disbelief that we witness these unusual events. The melting process continues. A red color seems to be on the ground and in the air. We believe red means the earth is red hot by now!

Passing over the ocean gives us a reprieve for our eyes. Our pain and suffering is still ongoing, but not seeing the terribleness of the land and all thereon is a break, though we know it won't last very long. When North and South America come back into view, I ask you, "How much worse will things be?"

You answer, "I am afraid to guess!"

If this process continues, the earth will soon be like a star or sun—just a ball of hot gases! Nothing of the earth's surface will be recognized as oceans, mountains, hill, or valley. All will become one.

Sure enough, just as we feared, our land where we had lived is not recognizable. In the distance, ashy, red, and even a few blue places are visible in the fire and melting rock and dirt. A few skeletons of buildings and monuments are standing, although we wonder for how long. Crying and moaning over what we had once possessed is all around us. Knowing our comforts are all burnt up has a way of overwhelming our being.

Up north, way up north in Canada and beyond—clear to the North Pole—the ice has almost all melted, and we see the depth of the earth as no man has seen it before. Much of this land had been covered with snow and ice all the time. Now even the coldest spots on earth will not last much longer. Steam is everywhere as the cold and hot mix.

Some wonderment overtakes me as I view the happenings below. It is becoming apparent that the earth is furnishing light for us to see. Remember back at the judgment how the moon became red as blood and we thought about how that was so very strange? Everything we know is different now. Many things seem upside down or backward or out of order. The order God established in the beginning of time has ceased completely. On earth, we experienced many troubling and out-of-place things but nothing even close to the catastrophes we are now seeing.

Genesis tells us the Holy Spirit of God moved upon the face of the waters. In the beginning the great Spirit of God caused creation, the creation of land and water, of light and darkness, of all that came to be. I wonder if in your wildest dreams, you ever imagined what we are now seeing. It must be that God's Spirit is gone. Maybe God has withdrawn beyond that great gulf He fixed, the one no one will ever cross.

"Are you still thirsty?" I ask.

Please don't answer because if you are not, I would feel tormented more than you, and if you are, then I know the feeling! Feelings, I believe, are going to be a very big part of our suffering. If feelings would cease, the torments would be much less. How, oh, how can we lose our feelings? If you come up with any solution, please let me know.

We continue, and the Atlantic Ocean approaches. This time, there are spots of land showing. The water is disappearing very fast. The water that remains is boiling and steaming. The land showing through is red hot. Every creature of the sea has come to naught. Sometimes it even appears as though some of the water is on fire. Can you believe that? Remember, the rules have changed. What could not have happened before can happen now! With God, all things are possible! We never saw this part of Him before! His greatness was enjoyable before. He gave us many blessings with His love while we were on earth. In hell, without His presence, without His greatness helping us and without His love abiding for us, we have no hope, no comfort, and no peace!

Then after the ocean, land comes into view again. The sight is unspeakable.

Everything on the land below is gone—no buildings, no trees, no rocks, nothing. The mountains have melted, and the valleys are filled up. All we can see are hot gases and exploding red-hot flames. The flames are towering. They engulf the devils, and they are about to reach us. The screaming and moaning reaches a new level. We surely know now that *hell has begun!*

The cries become, "Oh, please, don't let this terribleness become any worse," and we realize no one who can do anything about our troubles can hear us! On and on we go, over and over we roll, up and down like a yo-yo, tossing and turning, begging for mercy with none to be found. We can't explain any land masses to you anymore. All boundaries have become blurred, and we don't know where we are. The only recognizable landmarks are the poles, and we can say that both the North Pole and the South Pole have melted. Extreme heat is pouring out from them. We must now come to the conclusion that our earth has become like the sun. We used to know that no one in the flesh would be able to survive. However, our incorruptible bodies do not breathe or eat; they will live on forever. They will always be thirsty.

The flames, the eternal flames, are now leaping so high that we are engulfed by them. The burning is unbearable, and yet we have to bear it. The pain is beyond belief, and yet we have to believe it. The suffering is inescapable, and our doom is terrible. Yet I believe it may still get worse. If someone cared, the pain might seem more like a cloud-nine experience to us. If someone cared, the pain wouldn't be so great. If someone cared, maybe we could bear it. But no one cares, and we must bear it anyway.

I ask you, "Do your eyes burn? Mine do, and I don't believe they will take this brightness much longer."

You reveal that yours likewise are burning from the brightness. It all becomes so real to us that everyone is experiencing the tremendous brightness and all eyes will be burned out. In a short time, all will become dark, so dark the Bible said it will be outer darkness; (Matthew 25:30).

And then it happens! So dark, falling in the bottomless pit of hell without direction, amid weeping and gnashing of teeth. So dark! So dark!

Oh, for one ray of light!

Scripture References for Chapter 2

1. Revelation 1:18
2. Matthew 25:41
3. Luke 16:26
4. Revelation 21:27
5. Hebrews 11:25–26
6. John 15:20
7. Isaiah 5:14–15
8. Judges 10:13–14
9. John 8:44
10. Revelation 6:12
11. Genesis 1:4–10
12. Matthew 19:26
13. Romans 5:5–8
14. Matthew 25:41–46
15. Revelation 20:10–15
16. Matthew 8:12
17. 2 Peter 3:10–12
18. Luke 12:48
19. 1 Peter 1:18–19
20. John 1:10–12
21. Matthew 5:10
22. Luke 3:15
23. Acts 17:22–31
24. Matthew 25:41
25. 2 Peter 3:10–12
26. Genesis 1:2
27. Genesis 6:3
28. Mark 10:27
29. 1 John 2:15
30. Luke 16:24–25
31. Luke 12:5
32. Matthew 25:29–30

CHAPTER 3
THE PHYSICAL SUFFERING OF HELL

P HEW! WHAT IS THAT awful smell? I am choking, and you are losing your breath. This smell is killing us. We are in trouble indeed!

"Brimstone! Brimstone!" you say.

Yes, the Bible told us there would be a lake of fire and brimstone. It is plain to our senses that we are in that fire. The melting earth or burnt-out sun must have caused an extreme amount of sulfur, and I wonder how we can survive this calamity. If we still had earthly bodies, it would be certain death, and if we could have death now, it would be welcome … very much so!

Well, it has become clear: eternal death means dying but never dead. It means always coming back to suffer some more, where the worm dieth not and the fire is not quenched; (Mark 9:44, 46, 48).

"Do you have some nose plugs?" I ask. "Why didn't you prepare for this? We could have brought nose plugs, earplugs, breathing masks. We surely could use them now."

Our senses are working overtime. They are trying to keep

up and bring us as much comfort as possible. The big problem is that we have nothing to work with. There isn't any way to better ourselves. And of course, not seeing because of the tremendous darkness is also a hindrance. So the fire burns on! This lake seems to be everywhere.

"Plug your nose! Plug your nose!" you scream.

A cloud of burning brimstone is floating toward us. If you breathe it in, it will burn your insides as well as your outsides. The cloud is a thick, toxic vapor. Please, God, don't let another one like that come our way! The moans and cries float in from everyone, and I yell, "Quiet!" and then, "God, please stop this!"

You exclaim, "Don't you know God doesn't hear us anymore?"

"Yes, yes," I respond. "But can't I hope?"

"Hope, hope, I wish," you answer.

Hope was over long ago. Remember when the trumpet sounded? Yes, well, that's when hope ended, and I mean it ended forever.

Thirst is ever-present. We've been thirsty so long that we have forgotten how water tastes and satisfies. Our tongues feel swollen and parched. Our teeth are so dry that they seem to crack in our mouths. A drop of water would seem like a river! A river would seem like an ocean. I'm telling you and whoever will listen that just a little water would satisfy if we could have some. A cool tongue would be a gift from heaven, but as with the rich man and Lazarus, there isn't a way across the great gulf that is fixed. That means no one will bring us water! And so we suffer on. What else can we do?

We hear shouting in the distance, terrible moans and troubled begging. When the voices become clear, we realize another cloud of vaporous brimstone burning with vengeance is coming.

"Get ready. Plug your nose," you say.

Just in time, I get my burning fingers (whose tips feel raw and partly gone) up to block the vapors. "I'm not sure I can stand another one of these episodes," I answer back.

The fire is very painful and troublesome, but it is mild compared to the burning brimstone.

The taste in my mouth is awful, maybe somewhere between rotten eggs and green persimmons. We wish that we could report something good or something going well. We can't. There isn't anything uplifting or enjoyable about this place. Our troubles on earth were minor indeed compared to what we are experiencing now. The worst experience one ever had on earth would seem glorious and pleasurable compared to this place we now suffer. If you died at the stake, like some people did in the days of persecution, maybe then you would somewhat understand our experience, except we are falling all the time, and knowing this will go on and on without end makes it a much more horrible experience.

This bottomless pit is beyond imagination. There isn't any stability here. If we could lie down and rest for one night, we would grin from ear to ear. If someone would provide a chair to sit on, we would feel refreshed. If we had a platform to stand on for one hour, that would be great. If we could just grab hold of something solid for a moment, then this falling feeling could stop temporarily. Did the astronauts experience these falling and weightless feelings in space walks?

They had tethers to bring them back. Our experience here is like theirs but without any way to hold on or bring oneself back.

Hell's environment is burning torments and being alone without any hope or way to be helped.

Can you grasp how tired we are? Can you feel our pain? Can you comprehend the aloneness and hopeless feelings we have? We will never hold a glass of cold water again. We will never experience the joy of eating a wonderful meal with loved ones again. We will never feel the heartbeat of a loved one close by our side. We will never hear these words: "I love you." Never again will we see a beautiful sunset, rain falling from the sky, flowers blooming, or rows of crops gracing the fields of farmers. No more seeing the mountains, rowing down the stream, riding a bike, walking on trails, or sightseeing. Never another hug, compliment, greeting, handshake, or coffee break. We will not experience naps, dozing off, resting in the recliner, or just enjoying an evening at home. We won't have any more visits with friends, births, meetings, or heart-to-heart sharing. All this wouldn't be so bad if we would have the joys of heaven, which would bring us greater joy, joy far beyond the pleasures of earth. In hell, all good, all joy, and all hope is over.

The burning of our bodies, and especially, our extremities—hands and feet, toes and fingers, noses and ears—brings screams and moans. These noises seem to be coming from every direction. As the pangs of hell continue to torment our beings, the pain becomes beyond what we ever thought mankind could bear. Adding to the torment is the fact that we here are all in the same boat. No one can help each other. No one can help him or herself either. On earth, it seemed like there was always a way to improve our situation. Hell offers no improvements, and because God has turned His back on us, we can't even hope for a better environment.

We have a little longer break this time, but we are afraid the brimstone will be coming back. Sure enough, it's here! Thick clouds, burning and rolling, taking our breath away, giving us another lesson on how foolish it was for us to turn our backs on God and His Holy Spirit. Oh, oh, if only I could live over again. I can promise you I'd be the best Christian I could possibly be. I would listen closely to hear God's voice. I'd read the Bible daily. I'd love God more than anyone or anything. I'd love my fellow humans and treat them like I would want to be treated. I'd pray every day and have sweet communion with Jesus and God. I'd go to church on time, and I wouldn't miss unless completely necessary. I would surely try to help others to be saved and to avoid this awful place called hell! Yes, I would accept Jesus as my personal Savior—the free gift God gave for whosoever would accept Him. If I had it to do over again, I promise I wouldn't be here.

The list of our needs is long, and it goes on and on." Will you report some of our most urgent needs?" " Yes, we need lotion for the tops of our heads. The hair has burned off, and it feels like a severe sunburn up there. Of course, it would be better if we could have our eyes so that we could see again. This complete darkness is very depressing, and on top of all our other troubles, it is really getting us down. Our noses are sore and burned; something to ease the pain there would be appreciated. Our lips are dry and cracked; some kind of lip balm would help. The tongue and mouth and the throat and teeth are all dried out and—we've said this before—water, having some water is on our minds all the time."

The arms and hands are driving us crazy. It feels like we have severe cases of poison ivy, burning and itching; some calamine lotion would surely help. Our backs are taking a beating too. Our backs feel like we've been beaten with whips. We need someone to pour in oil and wine like the Good Samaritan of the Bible. We need help, but we have come to believe by now that no help will be available.

Our legs and feet have no useful purpose, but they are another source for pain. I hear you say it feels like a severe case of athlete's foot, and I share the same sensations. So now we need anti-itch lotion or spray and some cool air blowing on our feet. Our legs are sore and tired and burning. They have been working and squirming and slithering. We wouldn't know what to ask for to comfort them. We wouldn't receive anything anyway, so what's the use? The nightmare is ongoing. Hell is unrelenting, and hearing the singing of heaven now and then only makes the suffering worse.

Between missing heaven, having those clouds of brimstone engulf me, and the terrible pain that is more than my body can bear, panic attacks overwhelm me. I know fretting and worrying will only make things worse, but I can't help myself. Being completely beside myself not only agitates me but you and others as well. Like a fire spreads, so our feelings spread, and the more someone is bothered, the more everyone seems bothered.

Like trying to sleep when someone nearby is snoring, the groans and wails are another punishment of hell's tentacle-like arms. They keep bringing us into the swallowing abyss of hell. We would like to tell some of our fellow tormented to be quieter; however, we can't see them, and besides, we wouldn't know where to direct our request. It is becoming clear to me that the panic attacks will become worse and become another one of hell's terrible punishments. To be comfortable would mean so much.

Just knowing of Lazarus in Abraham's bosom grips the heart and soul. Like a blow of a hammer to the head, the reality of our situation is reinforced over and over again.

I knew it. I just knew it. The panic just struck you. You are screaming and screaming. You are totally beside yourself.

"Be quiet!" I say. "Be quiet!"

Your response is to scream louder. I wonder how you would look if I could see you now. On earth, you would have been very embarrassed to act like you are acting now, but in hell, it doesn't seem to matter what others think about anything they do or say. The only thing on our minds is how we can try to ease our sufferings and wonder why we ended up here, blaming ourselves because we didn't prepare for eternity, saying over and over, "Had I only, had I only."

My mind considers, and I believe I have just figured out what went wrong. The picture of earth's life had been in 3-D. I saw the outside picture, and it looked so good. Pleasure and fun, going and doing, living and joking, having and telling, and repeatedly living it up—life to the fullest! I hardly considered sin or what it was and where it would take me because the outside picture looked so good. Why should I think anything would or could go wrong? Why would I think I could possibly end up here? How could I think hell would really be real? Our conversations agree. Our puzzlement seems united. Our intentions were never to forsake God and His way.

And yet that little voice that spoke inside my heart tried to tell me. I heard a call, and I've come to realize that inside the earth, life's picture was another picture, a very different picture, a lowly way, one not pleasing to my earthly self. It was a narrow path that would lead to heaven. It was a picture of Jesus, the cross, confessing, being humble, turning from and forsaking sin. I didn't see it. I didn't want to look. I sure didn't want to strain to see and put forth much effort. The lowly way looked hard, and it seemed you couldn't do many things you wanted to do.

The terrible screaming starts again. Down the way over yonder, I hear excited voices, bloodcurdling cries, groans of misery, and shouts that pierce my soul. I know that as these many miserable sounds get louder, whatever is causing them must be coming closer. The smell of the air, the extra heat, and the burning feeling tells me all I need to know. Again, the burning brimstone cloud is here. Panic and fear, wondering how bad and how long it will last, blast me like sand being shot out of a high-pressure device. Wounded and weary, I wonder how I can take it. Listening to you and others make unearthly noises beyond what human ears could stand causes me to cry like a baby.

As if being sorry now would do any good, I become very repentant. Hope is gone except the hope that we make it through this vaporous cloud. Of all those clouds that come throughout eternity, knowing that God left us in the darkness is very hard to accept. On earth, He was such a loving God. He was ready to forgive us over and over again. Now His presence is gone, and no one in hell will ever be forgiven. The beat goes on! This time, the brimstone is even more unmerciful. The hot cloud seems to be sticking to us and burning more and more. I hear you say, "Let me die. Let me die."

We all feel that way. Death would be the easy way out of hell. Death would be my friend if he could come and take me.

I remember a verse from the Bible. It said something about a worm not dying and the fire not being quenched. I ask you, *Does that mean us? Does that mean this terrible life we now have is forever? No! No! It can't mean that, can it? Won't we eventually burn up and be gone?* The answer to our questions (though we should have known them) comes in a most unpleasant manner. While we listen with our ears, we hear a great voice. It comes from over by the great gulf that is fixed between heaven and hell. The voice says, "Doomed forever … and forever … and ever. Amen."

The 3-D picture comes back to me. The Bible stories heard at mother's knee is part of that inner picture. The still, small voice of God speaking to me is also part of that inner picture. But because I grieved and didn't obey God's gentle, prompting voice, I didn't see in 3 D. I neglected the spiritual part inside of me, whose needs I should have provided for even before the needs of my human body. I didn't grasp the picture inside the picture, and instead of following the right way, I followed my own thinking and did as I pleased. And that is the reason why I am here in hell.

The Bible tells about a foolish man who built his house on sand. He was foolish because he didn't build upon a stable substance. We did just that by rejecting Jesus, the rock, the only stable place to have built on when eternity broke.

There is no swearing here that we can tell. In one way, it seems people would blame God for all this suffering and terribleness. But it doesn't seem to be happening. It must be that everyone realizes God did His part. He freed Himself, and instead of blaming God, everyone is blaming themselves. We are all remembering the chances we had to be saved. We know that God made us people of choice. He never forced anyone to repentance, and therefore, He left the choice up to us. It is very sad to say we made an exceedingly bad choice, though we didn't think taking our own way would ever bring us here. (One surely never thought it would be this bad.) We trusted too much in our own good intentions and hoped God's mercy and love would overlook our wrong decisions.

The Bible said it plainly, but we excused ourselves for many reasons, like those in the Bible's parable who were called to the wedding supper that was prepared for them. The Bible says because of their own reasons, they made excuses, and therefore, they couldn't come. All of us here in hell chose by our decisions of rejecting the great supper invitation of salvation to be here, and though it is hard to admit that we failed so miserably, it has become clear that we cannot blame God but that we have only ourselves to blame!

"Will we ever get used to this torment?" you ask.

I wonder the same thing. *Will hell ever be routine?*

Roll up, roll up! Make yourself as small as possible. We are being sideswiped by a big vaporous brimstone cloud. The heat is rolling off it in circles, and the fumes are toxic and tortuous. The smell is beyond awful, and the flames leap out at us like dragons. They seem very mad! Intense pressure is building, and our bodies feel like we could just blow apart. Wails and screams are approaching many decibels. Our ears are ringing, and we must admit this is the worst, most monstrous, mountainous, gaseous, and gigantic cloud of brimstone burning yet!

The devil, it appears, has just released a terrible cry. He is so far to the left. Just imagine, he was once in heaven, and now he is in the depths of hell, the very worst possible place in hell, where he shall remain forever. It's not that we feel sorry for him. Nor do we know if we feel sorry for others. The torment is so great that we seem to think only about ourselves and why we chose this place. How could we change our situations now?

Doom hasn't quite sunk in yet. Doomed means accepting our

punishment. Doomed means there is no hope. We are almost at that place because God has left us and He has severed our souls from Himself. Jesus doesn't intercede anymore, and improvement looks impossible. So, again, the questions remain: "Will there ever be any improvement to our suffering? If God doesn't help us, who will?"

On earth, we had countless helpers: doctors, policemen, ministers, lawyers, presidents, counselors, businessmen, fathers, mothers, siblings, relatives, and many others. These people can't help us here. Some went to heaven, and those who are in hell with us have no eyesight or tools to work with or medicines to help soothe our pains. They can't even help themselves.

We are coming to know a place like no other. We could never have understood what we are experiencing. There is no way we could have foreseen hell's terribleness, no way we could have comprehended its boundlessness, and no way we could have imagined its torments. But we would not have had to come here! We were told of the two destinies, heaven and hell. All of us here chose hell!

We were very foolish!

Scripture References for Chapter 3

1. Revelation 19:20
2. 1 Corinthians 15:52–54
3. Jude 13
4. Matthew 25:41
5. Revelation 22:11
6. Matthew 8:12
7. Luke 13:27–28
8. Revelation 9:2
9. Ephesians 2:12
10. Romans 1:21–23
11. 2 Timothy 2:15
12. Luke 6:31
13. 2 Corinthians 13:14
14. Psalms 122:1
15. John 3:5–7
16. Revelation 15:3
17. Ecclesiastes 11:9
18. 1 Kings 19:12–13
19. 1 Corinthians 7:17
20. Matthew 7:14
21. 1 Corinthians 1:17–19
22. James 4:10
23. 1 John 4:7–8
24. Matthew 25:46
25. Isaiah 30:21
26. Matthew 7:26–27
27. Romans 1:20
28. Luke 14:16–22
29. Ezekiel 18:4
30. Revelation 21:8
31. Mark 9:44
32. Matthew 18:8
33. Revelation 19:11–16
34. Luke 16:26

35. Matthew 25:29–30
36. Revelation 14:11
37. Revelation 16:10
38. 1 Corinthians 2:9
39. 1 John 4:1
40. Matthew 22:37–39
41. 1 Thessalonians 5:17
42. Psalms 23
43. 2 Timothy 4:2
44. Luke 10:34
45. Matthew 13:42
46. Matthew 25:44
47. 1 Samuel 3:9–11
48. Ephesians 4:1–2
49. John 1:29
50. 1 John 1:9
51. Luke 14:33
52. 2 Peter 2:17
53. Revelation 20:10
54. Proverbs 14:12
55. 1 Corinthians 10:4
56. Hebrews 11:25
57. Luke 10:18
58. Matthew 7:13–14

Chapter 4
The Mental Suffering of Hell

W E'LL SOON BE EXPERIENCING the very worst part of hell. I can feel it coming. My mind is racing to past opportunities. I could have accepted God's way instead of misjudging and belittling. Did you think of God being much bigger than you were? Did you think He knew so much more? Did you see Him as being in control of all things visible and invisible? Maybe it seemed like we had the answers to life's problems and we could take care of ourselves. Could it be that we are here because we trusted in our own understanding and made our own decisions? I wonder if we really believed the Bible. If believing means following instructions and obeying, would we be here now?

We surely didn't understand how great and powerful God is, but we definitely comprehend it now. The Bible told us that heaven was His throne and the earth His footstool. What? You mean the whole earth was so insignificant that all of the land and all of the water, including the oceans and lakes, were as God's footstool? If that's the way it was, then the oceans weren't even big enough to be God's bathtub, though He never needed a bath. If the whole earth was as His footstool, one step of God's would span much of the universe. While He is sitting on His throne in heaven, His feet reach the earth, so it's no wonder He could hang the stars so high, put the planets in their places, and completely confound the wise. If we had understood before what we understand now, how different our reward would be. If we had understood His power like we understand it now, we wouldn't be here in hell.

God was all over. His power and reach spanned from eternity through eternity. The earth, our dwelling place, was only a very small part of God's habitation. "He inhabiteth eternity;" (Isaiah 57:15), the Bible said.

Here comes someone. He is speaking about being an atheist. "Grab a hold of him. Here he comes. I'll get one hand. You get the other! We must interview this fellow. You got him! Great! Hey, buddy, your hands sure are hot! Why are you here? For what reason do you think hell was your destiny?"

"I was an atheist!" he says. "I chose not to believe in God, but I sure believe in Him now. If it weren't too late, I can tell you … I would believe, and that is for sure! My mother taught me the right way. She tried her best, and I'm sure she is in heaven now. Somehow, education and science grabbed hold of me, and I forsook my upbringing to believe all things must be proven and explained. I was a fool. I was a fool. How could I have been so foolish?"

Then he asks us why we are here. We, too, tell him how foolish we had been and that though we had believed in God, we had just taken life casually, done our own thing, and hoped God would be merciful. We knew we hadn't repented of our sins and given our all to God. We just took the easier way then, but now this is surely not the easier way. The way of the cross was for "whosoever," and that included each of us and everyone else.

Then He left this thought: *God was and is real!* He is so big and powerful there is nothing too hard for Him. What we are being tormented with now is the power of God. He has put us here in this place of punishment, and no one or anything can change what will happen.

"So long, fellow. We wish you the best. Thanks for the interview, and if you find some comfort, let us know. We long to be comforted and relieved of this pain and terrible suffering."

As he floats away in the bottomless pit, we come to know there are many souls all around us. Though we can't see them, we know by their moans and groans and crying voices that many are experiencing the same torments we are. It seems like some comfort would come from having lots of company. That is not the case.

It has become very plain to us. There is no power but God's power. In eternity, everything is happening as He said it would. The devil is helpless. All men are helpless, and the footstool God set on fire is burning and will burn throughout eternity. No one can stop it or do anything to change what God has done! His greatness is being understood now. The sad part is that it's too late, too late ... yes, too late.

The very worst part of hell is that God took all love with Him. Love is not here. Feelings for others have left us. We never realized that love on earth held everything together. Though hate was on the earth and we saw it many times, love abounded much more. Families loved each other. People cared about other people. Someone was always ready to help. Doctors treated the sick. Hospitals tried to keep their patients comfortable. Policemen protected citizens when they knew of hostilities. Many deeds of kindness were done. God's love made the earth a pleasant place. God's love was all around us, starting from the moment of our birth to our dying day. God's love had a way for us. If we had followed His way, we wouldn't be here. Still, He didn't give up on us. His love kept calling us to Him. Over and over, His calls tried to bring us to the heavenly way. The mental part of coming to the realization of a forever without love causes us grief beyond human understanding.

"How will you ever bear a loveless place?" I ask.

"I'm scared," you answer. "I can't even imagine a complete lack of love."

Mothers in heaven won't even miss their lost children. Your mother won't even remember you, because knowing your suffering would cause her grief and tears and the Bible said there wouldn't be any tears in heaven.

If your mother were here in hell, you wouldn't have any love from her either. She wouldn't know you from any other person. Complete darkness would hide your face, and if light would be shown on you, I wonder if anyone could even tell who you are. How much different do we look because of the pain and suffering we've come through? Surely, this terrible experience has taken its toll!

The Bible has said God is love. Doesn't that mean wherever God is, there is love and that wherever or whenever God has left, there is no love? That seems to be the situation we find ourselves in. To be without love in earthly life would have been very stressful and miserable. To be without love in hell is beyond any words we can speak. It is a terrible place, and all the bad descriptions we could say don't even start to give a real picture of this abyss. As the brimstone was much worse than the fire, so being without any love is worse than the brimstone. I know and you know that is saying a great deal because the brimstone almost killed us. (We wish it would have.) To say love's end is worse comes from within. Remembering back to love and being loved is a feeling that goes beyond physical suffering. It is suffering from the heart. From deep within our souls, we are suffering, suffering, and suffering!

Hell has taken all my friends and your friends. Caring was another part of love. On earth, we gave because we cared, we helped because we cared, and we consulted with others because we cared. We hugged. We dreamed. We went places. We talked, and we did kind deeds for each other. All such pleasures are over.

In our earthly life, God created us as creatures of love. We were born with the capacity to love. You never had to tell yourself to love your mother. Unless she misused you in terrible ways, you loved her. She did so much for you. God loved you even more. He loved you so much. After mankind sinned and separated themselves from God, God prepared His Son, Jesus, to die on the old, rugged cross for our sins. Even before the foundation of the world, before God created earth and man and He knew mankind would sin, Jesus had accepted being the sacrifice for sin, the atonement, the bridge across hell so that we didn't have to come here.

The soul God gave us came from heaven. It was a part of God. We were all His children. We were His children until we chose to be disobedient and separate ourselves. He longed for us to be in heaven with Him.

"How could I have spurned love like this? Why did I take my own way?" someone asks.

"Couldn't God could have brought us to heaven anyway?"

The biggest mistake of mine was to believe thoughts like

that. The Bible had told us sin would never enter there! The devil fixed that one forever. He rose up, and God cast him out. He was doomed for his pride and rising up against God. We were doomed because we didn't accept God's love in a life-changing way. We wanted our own way more. So here we are, our souls severed from God. He cut us off. He took opportunity away. We became doomed by rejecting His invitations to accept Him and be saved. Love is gone. Love is over. Love is no more.

Though I now know and you know, it is very hard to accept a loveless forever. To think one will never feel love again is worse than any possible experience. Multiplying our suffering is the knowledge that heaven is filled with love. Just think! We could have been there, too! Another torment, yes, knowing we should have been there. Having the opportunity, being told of Jesus, feeling love from the higher power, and rejecting His loving call is shaking me to the very core.

"Can anyone stop this thinking?" you ask.

If our minds would quit working, we wouldn't remember all the missed opportunities and chances we had. If we didn't know of heaven, we wouldn't have this contrast of such terribleness compared to such bliss. If our minds wouldn't bring back memories and the pleasantness of life, if our minds didn't keep reminding us of Jesus's tender calls, then some of the suffering could cease. Our emotions, the part of us that keeps telling and revealing our feelings, are indeed the torment of hell. We truly had blessings and goodness in life on earth. We could have had much more blessing and been in a place with pleasures forevermore. Instead, we've come to hell, where no one is blessed and where pleasures are a distant memory—a memory that is receding further and further away.

"Stop talking! Stop!" you say. "Let it be quiet for a while."

Okay, I will, but when the dull roar of eternity affects you, you will wish for any other noise than to hear the sighs and the groans of the lost. The roaring of fire and brimstone and the thuds of eternity will play on your mind, and you will beg for someone to talk.

So now we're thinking, *What more is there to say?.* The noises we hear are coming from hell's monstrous fires and others— except the noise in our minds is becoming louder and louder and thunderous. The more idle and neutral we are, the louder eternity speaks. It seems the more we try to be comfortable, the more comfort escapes us.

So you cry out, "Okay, okay, someone talk. Someone please talk." Filling my mind with something is better than listening to the sounds of eternity. What a terrible noise!

Like love, joy, too, has left us. The little things of life that brought joy are all gone. Children brought joy, and they are in heaven. Many people did kind deeds and favors for us; they brought smiles to our faces and joy to our hearts. Smiles have vanished. I don't recall seeing or feeling anyone smiling since the trumpet sounded before Hell began.

You blurt out, "There's nothing to smile about." The little pleasures of life that brought smiles meant very much. To have none of them is another torment of hell.

Peace is over as well. To have peace, there must be a certain quietness. The inward quietness—peace of soul and heart—is over because God is not here. We receive no help from Him. He doesn't care about us anymore. The void of soul cannot be filled. There is nothing here to fill it with. Only emptiness prevails. We receive no rest, and there are no moments of peace. I wish for peace. You wish for quiet. And we wish for rest, but to no avail. The outward peace seems obvious. Of course, it is gone also with all the fire and brimstone, screaming and groaning, and the outer darkness. Peace in hell could never happen. We know that moment will never come.

Gentleness and kindness have ceased because we have very little contact with one another. How can you be kind or gentle with someone when you can't see or feel them? These attributes have become non-items, although we know it wouldn't be this way if we could deal with each other. Without any love or peace or God to help us, hell would be a war—every person for himself. Do you think God made hell so dark and people so without control because of this fact? In hell, we mostly suffer alone! The bottomless pit keeps us off balance and out of control.

The experience of the judgment comes back to haunt many times. It plays on my emotions, the finality of Jesus telling me, "To the left side you must go."

I've heard those words ringing in my ears over and over again. You know, and I know. Thoughts of changes in our situation seem impossible. The finality shreds our emotions. We are so without. We understand tears won't fix anything. We've come to know the coldness of no love in the heat of hell. The trauma and shock in between the mental cold and the physical heat is a roller-coaster ride of drastic proportions.

"My mind," you say, "it feels like it may blow up any time."

I hear someone asking, "Couldn't God have given us one reason to rejoice? Hell would still be a terrible place and suffering almost unbearable if we had just one workable option. Why did He take it all away?"

And then feeling sorry for myself, I realize letting these

thoughts into the mind will only cause more suffering. If you can blame God for your being here, it will only cause more grief. So the mind goes round and round, blaming God and then putting the blame on ourselves, where it really belongs, and then thinking of how we could suffer less, wishing for water to cool our tongues, hoping for a way out. We can't help but to remember the good times on earth and the glimpse into heaven, where we saw indescribably good things. Knowing we have missed heaven forever, and that hell will be everlasting punishment tears us up inside. Now even our thinking is torment. How can we stop the mind and find relief?

We can't. We can't, and that is one very sad part. Nothing, absolutely nothing appears to relieve us. My mind has gone down every imaginable avenue and found nothing of a pleasant nature.

"I am totally without!" I hear you say.

We've explored hell and found nothing. We've found nothing! *I can't go on like this*, I think.

"It won't work. Something has to give. There is only so much a person can take. Let our minds snap," you say. "We would be so much better off if all we had to do was suffer. Then at least our torments would be less by letting our minds become neutral. That would be a blessing in disguise."

"Blessings are not in hell," a voice echoes from the distance. "You will never lose your mind!" it screams. "You will always think of the wrong choices you made. You will never find any comfort. You are here with no way out! All the doors are shut. All gravity ceases. In the bottomless pit, there is nowhere to go!"

Resign yourself. Resign yourself. Give up. What you see is what you get. Nothing you try to do will change the outcome. The order of hell is pain and suffering, physical and mental pain and suffering forever. You might as well get used to it, though we all know you can't. You might as well accept it, though we all know that will be very hard. You might as well bear it, though we all know that will be almost impossible. Hell is where the impossible becomes possible by the power of God, who cast us here, and lights the eternal fire and brimstone. He took every blessing away and left us mentally without throughout eternity ... forever!

Scripture References for Chapter 4

1. Psalms 92:5
2. Isaiah 55:9
3. Acts 5:29
4. 1 Corinthians 1:25–31
5. Revelation 21:8
6. Luke 13:3–5
7. Proverbs 14:12
8. Luke 16:25
9. Matthew 7:13
10. 1 John 4:6–8
11. Psalms 50:1
12. 1 John 1:5
13. John 3:16
14. Ezekiel 18:4
15. Revelation 21:27
16. John 3:3–8
17. Luke 16:22
18. Psalms 16:11
19. Romans 1:18–22
20. Revelation 9:1
21. Revelation 19:6
22. Proverbs 3:5–7
23. Acts 7:49
24. Isaiah 57:15
25. 1 Corinthians 3:18–20
26. Acts 2:38
27. Revelation 22:17
28. Revelation 18:15
29. Mark 9:44
30. 1 Thessalonians 4:1
31. Revelation 21:4
32. 1 John 3:23
33. Romans 5:11
34. Acts 26:19

35. Revelation 12:7
36. Luke 16:25
37. Matthew 11:28
38. Matthew 25:41
39. Luke 16:24
40. Revelation 14:10–11

CHAPTER 5
INTERVIEWS AND THE ETERNITY OF HELL

BEFORE WE EXCHANGE OUR ideas of how long we will be here, we will conduct some interviews with our fellow sufferers in hell. Experience and knowledge of the Bible will reveal how long our stay will be. "Do you think we could talk to others about the reasons they came to hell?" I ask.

"Maybe they will tell us about their besetting sins and why they chose to live in their sins and why they didn't repent of them. Maybe they will share the whys and why nots of their decisions." you respond. It is our belief that most of them along with us knew better than to live in sinful pleasures. Let's get started!

Because of the fire, the screams, and the dull roar, it will be hard for us to have conversations in this bottomless place. Somehow, we must catch our participants, so in the darkness, we must grab someone as he floats by. Put your arms out and get ready. I think I feel a presence—my ears just picked up a groan.

"I'll latch on to the next person floating by," I say.

"I'll help you secure them so we can talk"

"What is your name young man?" I ask.

The young man answers, "My name is Joe."

"Okay, Joe, why did you come here? Has the sins that kept you out of heaven been revealed to you?"

"Yes, yes," he replies. "I was a fornicator. I lived to have fun with the girls, and my lovers were many. We partied long and often. I lived the life, saying and experiencing, 'If it feels good, do it!' Consequences hardly entered my mind."

"Well, Joe, didn't a little voice ever tell you or a little feeling come to you, making you feel evil for your sins? Didn't you know of the Ten Commandments of the Bible and Jesus's teachings? He even said that if we thought about fornication in our hearts, then we would be guilty. The Bible only gave us liberty to be intimate with our husband or wife. Joe, really, didn't you know?"

"Well, I have to admit that after my actions, many times I felt empty, and yes, I knew something wasn't right. Though I didn't consider God very much, God did have ways of making me feel unfulfilled with my life. I should have known when He was speaking and changed my ways to a life for Him. I can tell you the trade was a very bad one. For a little fun, I now receive the damnation of hell. It sure looks different now."

"So, Joe," I say, "you now say that if you could relive your sinful life, you wouldn't. You mean that, Joe? You mean you really wouldn't live the same way?"

"Yes, I mean that. This brimstone, fire, and mental and physical suffering have surely convinced me that I was totally wrong. Not one day would be the same if I could start over again. There is nothing that changes your mind like this hell where we now suffer!"

A middle-aged lady has somehow heard our interview, and she has latched on and grabbed hold. She seems very interested in our conversation, so I ask her if she would be interviewed next. She answers yes, so I am compelled to ask her about her earthly life and course.

"Why are you here, Sharon?"

She hesitates and seems embarrassed. "I lived a secret life, though I was married, had a husband and children, and mostly led a good life with many pleasant times. I worked for a large company and traveled much. Many times while away from home, I wasn't true to my husband. I lived in adultery. Our company employees partied and celebrated many times. I felt bad about my actions often but couldn't seem to help myself."

"Why would you do that?" I ask. "Shouldn't you have stayed home or found a different job? Did you ever feel uneasy and unfulfilled while having a secret? Or did you kind of enjoy a secret life? Was God ever able to reach your heart? Did you feel a little voice telling you of the sin you were committing? Were the Ten Commandments known by you, and did you know of Jesus's teachings about adultery? Was hell in your plans as you thought of life after death?"

"Yes, yes, I know," she says. "I knew I should've stayed home or found a different job. I knew my secret was wrong and displeasing to God. I felt uneasy many times and sometimes even cried because of guilt, and yet I enjoyed my secret life in a fleshly way. God called, and I felt a drawing to Him many times. My heart was too hard to give up, and to change would take much effort, so I just lived for the present and hoped for the best. I had been taught and I knew adultery was a sin. A little feeling after the fling was usually there. An uncomfortable knowing inside scolded me terrifically. I had my chance. I was taught about Jesus and salvation. I knew I needed His forgiveness, and to obtain it, I knew I needed to forsake sin. I had read some of the Bible and liked to hear about the love of God. But the judgment part condemned me, and I skipped around to read only comforting passages. I had hoped God would be merciful, and no, I didn't intend on coming here. Is this place really final?"

Next, by luck, we are able to get a hold of two people, one a man named Jim and a woman named Sara. They are both from the other side of straight. They had lived gay lives, not knowing or having anything to do with each other. We will interview them together because they both lived in the same sins.

"The Bible spoke about this sin," I say. "Did you miss what the Bible said? Or didn't you care, Jim and Sara? Didn't nature itself teach you how wrong your deeds were? Was it your impression you couldn't change? Did you think God wouldn't help you? Why would you live this way and come here to hell? What are your thoughts now?"

Jim has a very repentant spirit as he reports his feelings from then to now. He tells us how he started down the wrong road. By accepting little feelings as they came, his thinking was changed, and he looked at things in a different way. He knew the Bible didn't accept his sin, and though he cared, he didn't care enough to change and straighten his life out. Like the rest of us here in hell, he just coasted along and hoped all would work out well. To all of our shame, we did not listen to that little voice.

Jim says, "I knew what I did was against nature. I wanted help but didn't know how to get it. God was far away because I didn't invite Him into my heart, and my way was very much too important. Now I wish I could have changed from the inside to the outside. I wish I would have given my heart to God and let Him make me a new creature!"

Sara's situation is a little different. She grew up and followed the way her mother lived. She didn't know as much about God as

Jim did. She says she never read the Bible and hadn't heard much about God.

"I was at a real disadvantage to be saved," she says. "However, impressions and thoughts from somewhere else came to me. A feeling of being wrong came upon me when partaking of this sin. I think God was trying to tell me something, and it has become clear now. If I had listened to the impressions God gave me, He would have led me out of this sin and all sin. I believe God could have forgiven my sins if I had asked and repented. I do not blame God, but I hold myself responsible. As I ask throughout eternity, why didn't I follow those little impressions that would have brought me into the light and given to me heaven?"

Again, we are on the lookout, searching for another interview. We plan to find a murderer, a thief, someone who served strange gods, a covetous person, a selfish person, a boastful and proud one, an unbeliever, and an untruthful one. I hear a groan, and because we believe someone is close, we reach our arms out and snag someone.

"Hello, young man, how are you today, and what is your name?"

"I am George," he says. "I was a murderer. I killed people. I really got a big charge out of mastering them and controlling them until whoever I chose took his last breath. Jail was my home most of the time, and no one liked or thought well of me."

"Didn't you have any feelings, George? Wow, you must have been mean. George, did you care about anyone? Where was your mother? What about Jesus? Did you hear Him inviting you to salvation? Are you sorry now? If you had a second chance, George, how would you live?"

George starts crying (something he thought he would never

do). "I deserve hell!" he says. "I knew I would end up here. I never cared what others thought or felt. I was hard, but now I'm broken. Now it looks so different. God has taken all my strength and power away, and I can't do anything to help myself. I am being controlled by punishment far beyond what I gave. I wish I could die and have this terrible torment over with. It doesn't appear like that will happen, and I continually think, *Why didn't I change my life?* I had seen Christians while on earth, and I had no use for them. I hated everyone, but especially those who talked about God and Jesus. I loved myself, and nothing else mattered. I did what I wanted to do. Nobody could tell me anything. I was so wrong. I didn't think for a moment that hell would be this bad. The jokes and lighthearted talk of hell while living on earth made it seem bearable, and we strong and tough ones thought we could handle it. God has reduced us to less than nothing but won't even let us die. I wish I could live life over. I promise you I would be a Christian and I would never murder anyone or even think bad thoughts about them."

We are out of George's company now, and it seems like it would feel good to get away from such a fellow. (It doesn't.) No one seems more evil than the next one. All is evil, meaning all good has been taken away. Evil is what is left when you remove all goodness.

Next, we approach a group of sticky-fingered people. They were thieves on earth. This group stole many things. Let's be quiet and listen to them talk and fight to get away from each other. One of their punishments seems to be that they can't let go of anything. Their hands and feet are so sticky. They try to separate. Whenever one gets his hand free, his foot sticks to another one. They are pushing and shouting and kicking. Just when it seems one is almost free, another sticks to him again. Remember, there are men and women in this group, and it is very hot. Hell is always hot! Sometimes hotter than hot! We detect a cloud of brimstone coming toward us and them. We wonder what it must feel like to be consumed by these clouds, which are unbearable, and then be stuck together and kicked and hit at the same time. I'm glad I wasn't a thief. Again, we must conclude all are suffering, and it is not important to figure out who is suffering more.

The true God who sent us here told us from the Bible, "Thou shalt have no other Gods before me." We will now interview someone who served a different god. These other gods could be idols, things, beings, men, stars, or anything that is worshipped. The person we find in hell to talk to was serving a man-god or Antichrist.

Linda had a weak faith. It was hard for her to accept something she couldn't see with her eyes. When a man who called himself the "Son of God" was revealed, she became interested and joined his church. She liked being there, seeing, feeling, watching, and touching. She could accept that he didn't seem to have much more power than anyone else because he preached a way easy for the flesh. She could do just about anything she wanted to. There wasn't much of a cross to bear. Just bring money for the collection and live a good life. Entertainment was furnished at church—ball games, exercise rooms, feasts, movies, and most anything and everything for the members and whomever they brought with them. Her preacher never said she had to be born again, that she must change her life, putting off the ways of the flesh and denying herself. Her man-god preached that almost all would go to heaven.

She sometimes saw Christians who sacrificed many things for

salvation. She wondered, pondered, and questioned her Antichrist preacher. She finally chose to accept what she heard and thereby rejected many things the Bible said we must do. Linda tells us she is very sorry now that she hadn't accepted the real, lasting ways of her grandmother and grandfather, who believed in the true God. She says she now believes and is trying to find them here (in hell), but she doesn't believe they are here. She believes their true faith has taken them to heaven, and she is tormented by the fact that she, too, could have been in heaven if she would've followed their example.

A foul smell drifts over us, and I feel a presence near. As we call out, we ask, "Is someone here?"

"Yes," comes an answer. "You have Lloyd here."

"Hi, Lloyd. What do you have to say?"

"Well," Lloyd begins, "I was a big man, not in stature, but in goods and desires. I had stocks, bonds, real estate, gold, silver, and jewels, and I always wanted more. I did everything for gain. I coveted every good thing I saw—riches, honor, fame, people. I felt like I was owed. The way to gain was always wanting more and pursuing whatever means it took to get those things."

Lloyd stinks! We can hardly stand being here. It must be that God hates covetousness so much that He is giving extra punishment to those who committed this sin.

"Any other words, Lloyd?"

"I just wish I would have seen the important things in life and prepared for eternity. I know it's too late, too late!"

I listen and hear a squawky voice coming near. A woman who came to hell for what?

"Selfishness."

"Hey, lady, did you say you were selfish?"

"Yes," she says, "I am Kate, and I was selfish. Can you believe that I didn't care much for others, only myself—my needs, my wants, my desires, and mine, mine, mine. Everything revolved around me, and when I talked, you couldn't get a word in edgewise. When I drove, it was 'get out of my way!' When I played games, I was the best, and therefore, I should have the most of whatever. Wherever I went, it was 'I' and 'me.' People got tired of my lifted-up feelings, though I usually didn't know because all I saw was me. I wanted more than my share, took all I could get, helped myself first, cut ahead of others, gave myself pats on the back, and thought of myself always. Now I see the folly of it all. My motto should have been, 'Others first, Jesus first of all.' I should have been born into the kingdom of God. Then all things would have been in their proper order, and I would be in heaven now."

We call out for liars to respond, "Are there any liars within our hearing range?"

We get out of the way. Many are coming fast. Suddenly, we have a big group around us, many people who lied as though it didn't matter. They were men and women from all walks of life, every occupation. They used lies to protect themselves and others. Now those lies have backfired, and instead of protection, they, in part, have brought these people here to hell. Lies are part of a greater problem, and like all sins, they separate people from God. The tongue was one of mankind's greatest problems. Some of these people praised God with one side of their mouths and lied with the other side. The Bible said the truth would make us free. There is much crying and wailing. These people feel bad. They gave up so much to have so little (immeasurable doom), and if it would end sometime, there would be something to look forward to. It will not, and the mood is downcast gloom.

I wonder, *Do you think we can somehow get close to Satan?* Pride is our subject, and Satan is the father of pride. I believe he is near. Can you feel him, the greatest sufferer of hell?

"Satan, are you there? Can you hear us?"

"Yes." His voice is so weak we can hardly hear him.

"Satan, if you had the chance, if you could do it over again, would you try to overrule God and cast Him out of heaven?"

"No," comes the reply. "Never again would I rise up in pride if I had the chance. I was the most foolish being who ever existed. I had the glories of heaven. My angels and I are the only ones here in hell who know heaven. Pride took us down. Because of me, God said, 'No pride will ever be in heaven again.' Many are here in hell because of the pride of their hearts, and pride was one of the main temptations we used to deceive humans and bring them here with us. Pride made people seem like they were high up and noble. The Bible had told us there was nothing we had not received, and now we know how true that is. If we would be seen now, everyone would know. We have nothing to be proud of. The boastful are now quiet!"

Our last interview is coming up. We have found a man with the greatest sin. He didn't do much wrong. He wasn't the greatest sinner in deeds committed. He mostly chose not to believe.

"Don," I say, "why, why couldn't you believe the promises of God? We had it written in black and white. The Bible has stood through the ages of time. Men tried to destroy it. They killed Jesus, and He rose again! In a still, small voice, God has tried to speak to every one of us. Why, Don?"

"My faith. You know, I never saw God ... or Jesus. Yeah, I read some of the Bible, but you know, many people have written many stories. I can't accept the Bible just because it said 'God was.' Well, maybe He was, but what does that have to do with me? How do I know He cares? You know, I felt a little voice speak sometimes. Was that God?"

Don's questions went on and on. He had lived without believing and accepting God's way. Now in hell, he's here as one of the greatest sinners.

"Don, speak up. If you could live life over again, would you be able to believe?" we ask.

"Yes, yes, yes! Hell has a way of making me believe. I now know. There is no question in my mind. God has my attention now. If only it wasn't too late."

We've interviewed several people and heard their stories. Their stories always end, "Had I only repented—" It seems like we might feel better after we have heard others' experiences (like on earth), but it hasn't worked that way. We are not comforted. We don't know how long we've been here or how long this will last. (Eternity!) The only word that comes to our minds is doom! The fierceness and raging haven't let up. Nor does it seem like we have any reason to expect them to. The mind is our worst enemy, rolling over and over and over again. We just can't stop thinking, *Why, why didn't we prepare? We didn't have to come here.* That is so hard to know. We chose this place. God never made anyone become lost, but He did offer a way for everyone to be saved. The mind will keep taking us back—back to earth, back to the opportunity we all had, back to Bible stories on mothers' knees, back to the kind deeds we could have done. We think back to heaven, where some we know went, back to Jesus on the cross dying for our sins, and His blood being wasted for us, back to God whose love made a way even though man killed His Son. God gave each of us a soul (part of Him). Look what we did with it!"

These thoughts roll on and on and on. They will continue to roll. God will never let us forget. If we could, forgetting would be almost peace. On earth, we would go to sleep, resting our minds. In hell, there is no sleep. Our minds only stay engaged. This is torment.

Nothing can compare.

Scripture References for Chapter 5

1. 1 Corinthians 6:9
2. Hebrews 12:16
3. Isaiah 30:21
4. Hebrews 3:15
5. Exodus 20
6. Matthew 5:27–28
7. 1 Corinthians 7:1–2
8. Revelation 20:10
9. 1 Corinthians 6:9
10. Mark 10:5–9
11. 1 Corinthians 15:19
12. Luke 14:33
13. Revelation 20:13
14. Romans 1:24–28
15. 2 Corinthians 5:17
16. John 8:31–47
17. 1 John 3:15
18. Matthew 10:22
19. Matthew 24:9
20. Romans 1:25
21. John 3:3–7
22. Revelation 21:7
23. Exodus 20:3–7
24. 1 John 2:18–22
25. 1 John 4:3
26. 2 John 7
27. Luke 16:15
28. 2 Corinthians 5:17
29. Matthew 16:24
30. Matthew 7:13
31. Luke 12:15
32. Ephesians 5:3
33. Colossians 3:5
34. Hebrews 13:5

35. 2 Peter 2:10
36. Luke 6:30–34
37. James 4:6
38. Matthew 6:33
39. 1 Timothy 4:2
40. James 1:26
41. James 3:2–18
42. John 8:32
43. Revelation 12:7–10
44. 1 Corinthians 3:18
45. 1 Corinthians 4:7–8
46. Hebrews 3:12
47. Hebrews 3:19
48. Hebrews 4:6
49. Hebrews 4:11
50. 1 Corinthians 10:13
51. Luke 21:36
52. Hebrews 2:3
53. Hebrews 12:23–26
54. Genesis 2:7

Examine yourselves, whether ye be in the faith; prove
your own selves. Know ye not your own selves, how that
Jesus Christ is in you. 2.Corinthians 13:5

Verily I say unto you, Except ye be converted, and
become as little children, ye shall not enter the kingdom
of heaven. Matthew 18:3

But without faith it is impossible to please him, for he
that cometh to God must believe that he is the rewarder
of them that diligently seek him. Hebrews 11:6

Jesus answered and said unto them, ye do err, not
knowing the scriptures, nor the power of God. For
in the resurrection they neither marry, nor are given
in marriage, but are as the angels of God in heaven.
Matthew 22:29-30

CHAPTER 6
HOW WE GOT OUT AND THE
START OF OUR JOURNEY

SHOUT FOR JOY! JUMP up and down! Kiss the earth! Hug your mother! Hold hands with anyone! Love everybody! Pray now! Give yourself to God! Humble yourself! Accept Jesus! Lift your heads! Become God's alone! Reject the devil completely! It was a dream, a terrible, terrible dream. The downside of this dream is that hell will be much worse than our dream was.

Our experience was terrible. It was beyond suffering. It was more than persecution. We don't know how to act now. Urgency is on my mind. We have to do something to make sure we don't go to hell. We must find the escape route. Questions are coming fast. What do we do? Where do we go? How can we find salvation of the soul? The road that leads to heaven, the pathway, the narrow way! Grace, humility, peace, love, and joy! Our names written in heaven.

Listen! I hear the still, small voice calling out, the voice of God. "The Bible is your road map. The Bible is your road map.

Its pages have the answers. You will find the way to heaven, but you must accept all that it says."

There is no picking and choosing what we want to accept. Before this dream, we probably would have passed this voice off and taken our chances, hoping all would be well. Now it is not acceptable to have any such thinking.

"I know whatever I have to do, I will do it. The dream has shaken me to the core, and you surely feel the same way, don't you?"

"Oh, yes," you say, "let's get going and find our souls a good future home."

"How can we secure our mansion in glory, heaven? Remember, heaven is the only option. Heaven or hell—why such terrible extremes?"

"Hey!" you say. "Stop! There is no use trying to figure out why."

"Okay, you're right. We must get to work and find the answers to our end."

A name comes to me. "Jesus," I say. "Do you know Jesus?"

"Yeah, wasn't He God's Son, who died on a cross for the sins of all mankind? Whoever will accept Him as their personal savior must be the only ones God saves from hell."

"I think we had better get busy reading the good old book. We must study to see what we must do. You read, and when you have an impression, please tell me. And I'll do the same for you."

"We will study and listen carefully, because I remember hearing people talk about a whispering voice so small you had to listen to hear it. This voice was supposed to come from God! They said something about a trinity, three in one, something like God and Jesus and a voice being one and the same."

"Look, I started reading in Genesis," I say. "Here is the creation story. God is making everything. Just by commanding things to 'be,' they 'are.'"

"Wow, awesome power! Can you believe all this? He is just speaking things into existence."

"Here we go!" I start. "Right here it says how God made Adam out of the dust of the ground and he became a living soul. Look! It says Eve was made by taking a rib out of Adam, and just down the page here, it says God gave them one commandment. Don't eat fruit off just this one tree. Just one commandment—don't eat fruit off just one tree. Then a snake comes by and talks to Eve. Can you believe this? This snake is the devil and … hey! He gets her to take it, the fruit off the one tree! She eats it and gives some to her husband, and 'sin' has entered the world. That's why! That's why we had that awful dream of hell. God took them out of the garden, and they became sinners. And all who are born from their seed are sinners."

"These souls came from God, and He wasn't willing to just let them go to hell. Even before God made the earth, the Bible says He had a plan to save them, if they would let him. Jesus was this plan. Though God drove Adam and Eve out of the Garden of Eden, He still loved them."

"What are you reading?" I ask. "Did you find our answers? Tell me something. Psalms, you say. You are reading about David. He was a man after God's own heart. Surely, we can learn something from a man like that. What did he do to please God? If we can be like him, would that give us our passport to heaven?"

"Much praising and singing," you say. "He seems to hear God's voice, and when he commits sin, he doesn't excuse himself but has a humble and broken heart. Remember, David killed the lion and the bear because God was with him. Even as a youth, he seemed to have a relationship with God. He spared King Saul's life when he could have killed him. Though Saul would have killed David, and tried to, David didn't kill Saul, even though he had the chance, because he considered Saul to be God's anointed one. God gave David the giant, who defied God's people. A great victory was won that day. Where are you, God? Bring us beside the still waters and prepare us a table spread with the things that will save our souls."

"I just came upon the story of Noah," I continue. "Remember the ark, that big boat Noah spent 120 years making?

"He was commanded by God. Because of the wickedness of the people, God was going to destroy all flesh, except Noah and his family. Noah preached, but no one else listened. They made fun of him. Even when the animals came to the ark and went in, wouldn't that cause you to believe God's power was being revealed? Where were their senses? Why couldn't they understand? Why wouldn't they repent? Oh, God, have we been like them? Oh, God, help us to see!"

"I found another one!" you exclaim. "Daniel of the lions' den."

"Now here was a worshipper of God. It says here that a jealous man was trying to get rid of Daniel. He was going to use Daniel's religion against him, so this man went to the king and asked him to make a decree that no one could pray to God or anyone else for some days, and if they did, they would be thrown into a den of lions. The king thought very much of Daniel, but he didn't know that Daniel prayed to his God three times a day and did so openly at his window. The king, thinking the idea sounded good, signed the decree. Daniel, who loved God, kept praying. He wouldn't leave his God, even if it meant his life. Daniel was committed. His relationship meant more than earthly life. The decree couldn't be changed, so the king couldn't change his mind; therefore, he had to throw Daniel into the lions' den.

"But look! It says God shut the lions' mouths, and they couldn't do him any harm."

"Wow!" I say. "That is power!"

"The king couldn't sleep. So he came early to the den and called out to Daniel, 'Is thy God, who you serve continually, able to deliver you from the lions?'

"'Yes!' came the reply. 'God has sent angels to shut the lions' mouths.' Then the king had Daniel brought up out of the lions' den. And those who tried to do him harm were thrown in, and the lions broke all their bones before they even hit the bottom of the den. The decree was changed. Everyone must respect Daniel's God!"

"We know we must be committed," I say. "Next up, Abraham," the man God said would be the father of all nations. He didn't even have children until his wife, Sara, was way past the years of childbearing. God promised, and Abraham believed. He was the father of faith. Though his wife had some disbelief, Abraham believed God. After Isaac was born and grew to boyhood, God asked Abraham to take his son, his only son, the promised child whose seed was to become everyone from here on. One day, God told Abraham, 'Take your son up the mountain and offer him as a sacrifice to me.' When Isaac asked his father where the lamb for the sacrifice was, Abraham's faith said, 'God will provide.'"

"Can you believe this story? If I trust God like that, all will be well."

"Well, look here. It says Abraham had the lad on the altar,

lifting the knife to slay his only son, when God stopped him. In the bushes nearby was a lamb caught in a thicket. Together, Abraham and his son offered the lamb on the altar and went down the mountain rejoicing, their family still intact. Abraham proved his love to God, and God was satisfied with him."

"Lord, give me faith like Abraham," you say.

"After reading about Daniel, you read a little more, and what have you found, my friend?" I ask.

You continue, "Shadrach, Meshach, and Abednego."

"What … who … what do those words mean?" I ask.

"Oh, they were three Hebrew children who defied King Nebuchadnezzar—they disobeyed his command. You see, it says here that the king made an image of gold, an idol, and he demanded everyone must bow down and worship his idol. The music would be the sign for all to bow. The punishment for not obeying the king would be a hot, sure death. He was going to have whoever wouldn't bow thrown into a burning, fiery furnace. The music played, and the three boys wouldn't do it. Surely, they must have misunderstood. The king was mad, terribly mad. Somehow, through his madness, he still gave them another chance. Just imagine his wrath when they told him, 'We don't want another chance. We will not worship your image. The God we serve, the real God, can deliver us if He chooses to, but it doesn't matter. Oh, King, we will not defile ourselves with your god.'

"Red-faced, furious, beside himself, the wicked king commanded his most mighty men to heat the furnace seven times hotter than it should be heated. These men bound Shadrach, Meshach, and Abednego, tied ropes around them, and cast them into the furnace. The fire was so hot it killed the mighty men of Nebuchadnezzar. Now listen to this. The fire didn't kill the three Hebrews but only burned the ropes that bound them, and it appeared someone joined them in the fire. Four men were walking around, and the fourth one appeared like a being from heaven. The king changed his mind when these boys came out of the furnace and their hair wasn't even singed. Nor could anyone even smell smoke upon them. He then made a new decree. 'No one shall speak a word against the God of Shadrach, Meshach, and Abednego, or they will be cut into pieces and their house be made a dunghill, because there is no God like their God.' We want this God to join us and be our God!"

"Yes, we do!" I say. "Tell me what we must do. Whatever it takes, we must do, and we will do. The dream has us focused. It keeps us learning, and our studying will bring us to God. That is the truth we're grasping."

"Another experience still from Genesis is Joseph, the son of Jacob. It says here he had a dream. In his dream, others bowed down to him. This made his brothers very upset. They already hated him because it appeared to them that their father loved Joseph more, and now they were listening to more of Joseph's nonsense. Joseph had received a coat of many colors from his father, and these brothers had just about all they could take.

"One day after the brothers had left with the flocks to graze them, Jacob told Joseph to go and see how his brothers were doing, check on them, and come back to tell him. When Joseph finally found them, they saw their chance to get rid of this dreamer. Their plan was to kill him, dip his coat of many colors into the blood of an animal, bring it back to their father, and tell him a wild animal must have killed his son. The oldest brother didn't agree with this plan, but while he was away for a little while, some men came by. The plan changed, and they sold their brother Joseph to these men. The older brother was very unhappy because he had wanted to save the lad and return him to his father. Too late, so the plan must go on. The brothers dipped the coat in blood and brought it to their father, asking him if it was indeed Joseph's coat. Jacob mourned for many days.

"The story goes on, saying Joseph ends up in Egypt working for an officer of Pharaoh. Because he was a prosperous man and trustworthy, he became an overseer very quickly. It was unfortunate for Joseph that this officer's wife decided she wanted him for her pleasure. One day, she grabbed him, and he left quickly, leaving his cloak in her hands. She then lied about the matter, and Joseph ended up in jail.

"After much time, this dreamer interpreted some dreams for others. Pharaoh had a dream that troubled him very much. A bulter told the Pharoh about Joseph, who had personally interpreted a dream for him before, and Pharaoh called for Joseph to interpret his dream as well. Because God was with him, Joseph was able to reveal Pharaoh's dream about the seven good years and then the seven lean years. Because the lean years would need someone to prepare for them, Pharaoh decided Joseph was the man.

"And so it became Joseph's responsibility to save and store up for the famine. Some years later when the famine was severe, Joseph's brothers came to buy food from him. He knew them instantly, but they didn't know him. Joseph tested them to see if their hearts had changed. Finally, he revealed himself, and they were afraid. They bowed down to him just as he had dreamed many years before. Finally, the whole family came to the land where Joseph was. God was working this whole story out as He had planned."

"Does God have a plan for everyone?" I ask.

"There was a man whose name was Jonah. You are reading the story."

"Right," I say. "Jonah didn't want to do what God asked him to do (to go preach to the people). So Jonah started running away from God. He jumped on a ship heading in the wrong direction, found a place in the bottom, and fell asleep. God sent a storm that rocked the ship. The mariners were afraid. They asked the men on board to pray and tossed most of their supplies overboard. Then they found Jonah sleeping and decided someone on board must be responsible for this happening. After asking Jonah many questions and casting lots, they believed he was the man. The more he told them about running away from God, the more scared they became. Finally, they asked Jonah what they should do, and he told them to cast him into the sea and the sea would be calm. It took more rowing and soul searching before they became willing to throw Jonah overboard. When they did, the sea became calm, and unbeknownst to them, God had prepared a great fish to swallow Jonah. Three days and three nights, Jonah suffered down there. Like hell, he was without mercy. When his spirit changed and he became willing to do what God had asked of him, God had the fish vomit Jonah out onto dry land. Now he was willing to go and preach as God had commanded."

"This story is like our experience. We weren't willing before, but now we are!"

"Jonah was willing to go and preach when God asked him to after his fish experience; however, his selfish life soon returned. It seems unbelievable as you are reading this story that he could change so quickly. The story continues. Jonah went to preach, knowing that if the people repented, God might change His mind. That is exactly what He did as those people became very serious and repented. God spared their lives and didn't destroy their city. Jonah was exceedingly mad. His self-pity was destroying his relationship with God again. Only God knows what happened to Jonah."

"Help us, God, not to be disobedient and selfish," you say.

"Next, I found the Ten Commandments, written for God's children, His chosen people," I say. "These commandments lay down the laws of God, and if heaven will be our home someday, we must obey God's commandments. These laws are for everyone. Moses was God's chosen one by whom He gave the commandments on tablets of stone. God gave them to him on the mountain, and Moses was shining when he came down."

As I read on, I find Moses again. "Now Moses was born and should have been destroyed by the king's decree. He was hidden in a basket among the bulrushes and found by the king's daughter. Adoption into the king's family was God's way of saving Moses to lead the people of God to another land. He, with God's direction, delivered them out of the king's bondage. Moses decided to leave his life in the king's house with all its glory to suffer affliction with the people of God instead of enjoying the pleasures of sin!

"It looks like he took on a very hard job. The people Moses was leading had so many different ideas and disobediences, and because of these, they wandered in the wilderness for forty years. God worked so many miracles for them. They crossed the Red Sea on dry land, ate manna (the food from heaven), drank water out of a rock, and were led by God with a cloud by day and a pillar of fire by night.

"They made idols to worship, fell into fornication by the thousands, and complained constantly. Many of them died in the wilderness because of their sins. Disobedience made a very hard life for them when it could have been so much different."

"Job really had an experience," I continue. "God and Satan talked one day. God asked Satan if he noticed His servant Job. Now Job was rich in cattle and land and had a good wife and many children. He was upright and really had things going for himself. Job was very committed to God and His ways. While talking, Satan told God the reason Job was so faithful was because God had a hedge around him. In other words, Satan felt like he couldn't get to Job because God wasn't letting him. God agreed to remove the hedge, and things changed completely.

"Many troubles began. Some servants were slain. Oxen were stolen. Sheep were burned by fire falling from the sky. Camels were taken. Some of his sons were slain by a great wind, but Job remained true to God. He did not sin. Satan wanted more power, so God let him do anything to Job, except take his life.

"Boils appeared all over Job's body. Job's wife told him to curse God and die. Job's three friends came to comfort him. Job finally bemoaned the day he was born but also told his friends they were miserable comforters. Job wondered why all these things were happening to him, and he wondered why the wicked prospered. Instead of becoming bitter, he turned to God more and more.

"He finally submitted himself and abhorred himself, realizing God didn't owe him anything. Job said he heard of God, but now he had seen God. He repented in dust and ashes.

"He also prayed for his friends who had not understood. After Job's experience, God gave him more—twice as much as he had before: sheep, camels, oxen, seven sons, and three daughters. His daughters were the fairest in the land. Job lived 140 more years, enjoying all that God had given back to him and finally dying in old age. With the power of God and by not giving up, Job was blessed, and he is a good example for us. No matter how bad things become, if we are God's true children, there will be a way for us."

"I want you to know we must keep reading the Bible to find our way," I finally say to you. "Now we will start in the New Testament to travel with Jesus and His disciples and apostles. We need to come to the place God wants us to be so that we can love Him and avoid the terrible dream we experienced."

Scripture References for Chapter 6

1. Matthew 7:13–14
2. 2 Timothy 2:15
3. Genesis 1
4. Genesis 2
5. Genesis 3
6. 1 Peter 1:18–21
7. 1 Kings 19:12
8. 2 Samuel 11–12
9. 1 Samuel 17:34–36
10. 1 Samuel 26:6–9
11. 1 Samuel 17:41–54
12. Psalms 23
13. Genesis 6–8
14. Daniel 6:6–28
15. Genesis 18:6–19
16. Genesis 22:1–18
17. Daniel 3:1–30
18. Genesis 37- 40
19. Genesis 41- 44
20. Genesis 45- 48
21. Jonah 1- 4
22. Exodus 2- 6
23. Exodus 7- 11
24. Exodus 12- 16
25. Exodus 17- 20
26. Job 1- 6
27. Job 7- 12
28. Job 13- 18
29. Job 19- 24
30. Job 25- 30
31. Job 31- 37
32. Job 38- 42

Chapter 7
Understanding the New Testament

"HERE IT IS!" I say. "I know this is it! It has to be the answer, because it is written in red, so it means more. Doesn't that mean Jesus said these words?"

"Who is Jesus?"

"Why are you asking? Don't you know He is the Son of God and He came down from heaven, remember? Read the story and give me your thoughts as we study the ways of the Gospel."

"Wait!" you say. "Did you say He was born of a virgin? That's impossible! You must have made a mistake. No one can be born of a virgin."

"Yes, I did read that. The Bible says that. It's right here. See with your own eyes. Remember the faith we just studied in Abraham? You must grasp these words and believe. A miracle happened, and you must be prepared because we will read many more of them."

"So it says Jesus came to earth as we all did. He was born of a woman. The difference was how He was conceived—being conceived by God before Joseph knew Mary and before she

83

became his wife. Why did He come to earth is such a lowly way? He came that way because God chose the humble and quiet way. He is God's Son, the only one who can redeem us."

"You said a baby was born in a cattle manger. Yeah, right! The parents were traveling. The innkeeper had no room in his inn, but he had a manger outside with the cattle. The baby could be born there. Who would care? Are you telling me that a heavenly being came from heaven to earth and was born in such humility, where the cattle were his observers? That's outrageous!"

"We missed the clues!" you say. "We assumed honor, glory, riches, and fame—and here Jesus came with nothing. It's no wonder we missed the right way. Our eyes were looking way above the humble way."

"In the Bible, Simeon, an old man, knew who Jesus was, and when he saw Him and blessed Him, he told God, 'Now let me die, for my eyes have seen thy salvation.' Wise men from the East also came to see this Jesus child.

"Jesus grew with His family. It says here that it soon became apparent that He was a very unusual man. When He was a teenager or younger, He conversed with the most highly educated of the land. He could, because he had come from heaven. He knew all things, but the educated didn't know that."

"Look! Here's a sermon. Jesus is the speaker, and he is giving instructions, giving His blessings on some actions and His judgments on others. Where were we? Why didn't we know? The Bible has been sitting on my stand for years. In fact, I have several of them."

"Oh, check this out!" I say. "It says here that Jesus was in a boat when a great storm came up. The water was coming over the sides of the ship. His disciples were scared, crying out. They said,

'Save us! We will perish!' And what does Jesus do? He rebukes the wind and the sea and creates a great calm. Those with Him were amazed. They couldn't understand because they had never seen a person control nature like this before.

"Jesus cast out devils in people's lives several times. One day, there was a herd of pigs nearby, and the devils knew instantly when Jesus saw them that they must leave if He told them to, so they asked to be cast into the swine. Jesus told them to go, and the pigs ran down a steep slope into the sea and perished. Jesus's power was being revealed for a reason. No one else could command, and just by a word, He could bring whatever He said to pass."

"What have you found?" you ask. "Give me a parable that teaches us more. We are like hungry people who can't seem to get enough. Our experience has changed our desires. We believe that just around the corner, something extremely important will happen."

"Here's a parable of the prodigal son. Jesus used this parable as an example to bring us back to Him. One day, a man's son asks for his inheritance. He wanted to leave his father's house, go into a far country, and just do what he wanted to do. He enjoyed himself, and while he had friends and money, he 'lived the life,' wasting his substance in an unrighteous way. One day, it was gone—no money, no friends, and no God. In hopelessness, he cried out. He was so hungry that he wanted the husks the pigs ate, and nobody would give even that to him. Then he had an idea. 'I will return to my father in a very repentant way, and maybe he will forgive me and take care of me.' Jesus explained that the father was watching for his son to return, and the father did forgive him and take care of him."

"This story feels like our answer," you say. "It's what we must do to avoid the terrible agony and suffering we have just witnessed. It won't be easy, we know. It wasn't easy before, and we know that the devil will do all he can to keep us from returning to God. We have been extremely scared by hell, but another picture is entering my mind. It is the picture of love—loving He who saved us, giving to Him because He gave so much to us.

"We read another miracle in the Bible. It's a great event. Jesus divides bread and fish and feeds thousands. Wow! A little boy whose mother gave him a small lunch reveals that he has a few small loaves and fish. He seems to be the only person who has brought any food. There are thousands of people who have come to hear Jesus, but there is only a handful of food. What should the disciples do? Can someone purchase enough food to feed these thousands? No, Jesus has another plan. He was just waiting for this opportunity. Jesus instructs everyone to sit down on the grassy hillside. He prays to His Father, takes the loaves and fish, and breaks them into pieces, and then the food multiplies over and over again. The bread and fish are passed out. Everyone eats all they can, and what do you know? Many baskets of extra food are collected. We realize Jesus will do the same for you and me. He will supply all we can eat, and there will be plenty left for others."

"Here's another truth from God's Word," I say. "Picture yourself in a boat on the water at night in the dark. You glance over your oars and see a form walking toward you on the water. Jesus's disciples were described in this situation, and they were scared. They wondered who it was. They wondered if their eyes were deceiving them. They wondered if a spirit was walking to them. Peter called out to the form, and when it replied, it sounded like Jesus. It was Jesus! When Peter believed it, he said, "Lord, if it be you, bid me come," and Jesus said, "Come." Peter walked on the water until he started to look around. Then because his faith failed, Jesus saved him from perishing. Jesus may do the same for us when we need more faith."

"Here's a story about how Jesus brought a friend back to life," you say. "That Jesus had the power of God was difficult for the people of His time to grasp. Never had a man spoken with such power. Many didn't know how to take Him. Sometimes they supported Jesus, but then these same people wanted to get rid of him. His way was so different—so far beyond the way they thought—and this confusion has continued ever since. To change our thinking takes a power beyond what we have. However, God will help us."

"Here is some biblical information we must know," I added. "It's about the days when Jesus met the devil again. It happened in the wilderness for forty days. The devil repeatedly tried to tempt Jesus and cause Him to sin. The devil offered Jesus great power—the power of the world, the power of great honor, the glory of the world, and the power over the kingdoms of the world. The devil used the natural desires of man to try to tempt Jesus, but Jesus won every battle. He had the power to overcome the devil, and because of that, we have the ultimate opportunity."

"Listen to this story," you say, "during which Peter said, 'I am a sinful man, oh, Lord.' This day, the disciples had fished all day without success. They were ready to quit and give up. Jesus called out to them to cast their nets on the other side of the boat. The carpenters son told the fishermen how to catch fish. 'Okay, Lord,' was their response. 'But we want you to know that we have already cast our nets all day long without success.' When the fishermen obeyed Jesus, their catch was so great that their nets broke and they had a hard time trying to handle all of the fish. They had to call on others to help them. These disciples realized that Jesus had a greater power than their combined power. They felt the difference in a drastic way."

"Why would some people want to kill Jesus?" I ask. "He only committed good deeds. He loved everyone. He helped all He encountered. He told people the way to be saved and go to heaven. But some people hated Him without cause. Even those who followed Him couldn't see God's plan. However, Jesus knew why He came. He knew that some would want to kill Him. He knew that He would die. How could He be so kind, knowing what He knew? And here's more information. The Bible says that Jesus told His disciples what would happen to Him. He told them that He would die to be the sacrifice for all sin and then that He would rise from the dead. He told His disciples that He would return to heaven and send the Holy Spirit to lead His followers and to help them make the right choices. And finally, Jesus told them that He would come back to judge the world and take His children to heaven. But the disciples didn't believe Jesus. 'Surely,' they thought, 'our king will never die.'

"The day arrived. The time was close. Jesus knew. He tried to prepare the disciples for what would happen. We're now reading about the last supper that Jesus had with His disciples and His teaching about how to commemorate His death after He was gone. Jesus told them, 'One of you will betray me, and another of you will deny me three times.' The disciples would not accept Jesus's words.

"Oh, no. It's happening. Judas comes toward Jesus and gives Him a kiss. With sorrow in His heart, Jesus says, 'You betray me with a kiss. For thirty pieces of silver you sell me out!' The mob was there, and they wanted Him dead.

"In a few hours, the mob had won, or had they? Yes, Jesus died, or as He stated, He gave his life. The darkness in the middle of the day and many other unnatural events that occurred made the mob realize that indeed Jesus *was* different from any other man. One thief on the cross beside Jesus recognized Jesus as his Lord and said, 'LORD, remember me when thou comest into thy kingdom,' because he had a broken heart for the sins he had committed.

"Jesus responded, 'Today you will be with me in paradise.'"

"Our answer is right here," you say. "This is exactly what we must do. With God's help, we must be like that thief."

I continue reading, "At that time, many were disappointed. Some had spent years believing in Him and enjoying His kind and tender words and deeds. They had never seen hopelessness and despair because He had always had an answer and he had healed body and soul. Now He was gone—dead—and He hadn't even stuck up for Himself or called on the angels to deliver Him. Their king was dead! Or was He?"

"Listen to this," I say. "The Bible says that some women went to His tomb but it was empty. Instead, two angels were there telling the women, 'Jesus isn't here! He is risen!' This is too much. Change is happening too fast! The women make more mistakes because they refuse to believe the angels. Their minds are in a whirl. Within a few hours, some other disciples are claiming that Jesus had been walking with them after His death and that they didn't even recognize Him. They had been walking and thinking about Jesus's previous conversations with them when He simply appeared in their midst and said, 'Peace be unto you.' Now they are really frightened. Jesus calms them as He shows them His nail-pierced hands and feet. His disciples cannot grasp that Jesus is able to move about as a natural person. After He eats a meal with them, He opens their understanding about previous prophesies about the future and His return to heaven.

"Time passes, and then it happens. Jesus tells his disciples that He will send the Holy Spirit—the still, small voice—and this quiet voice will give direction to Christians everywhere if they will listen closely. While He is speaking, Jesus is lifted off the ground, rising continually. Many watch Him ascend, gazing at Jesus until they can't see Him anymore. And then His words come flooding back, and the disciples realize that they must now start His church on earth."

"Look!" I continue. "In the book of Acts, the Bible tells us about the day of Pentecost. Isn't it amazing how many were meeting together when a sound from heaven came down and filled each person with the Holy Spirit? Then with a unity of direction, the believers came together with one spirit in Christ, and Peter began preaching, 'Repent and be baptized, every one of you, and you shall receive the Holy Spirit and your sins shall be forgiven; (Acts 2:38). Three thousand souls accepted the invitations that day. These new believers were in agreement and pooled their common resources while they praised God and helped each other daily."

"I can tell that you have a thought," you say.

"Yes. It is really disappointing to realize that just as Jesus was mistreated, so His disciples would be also. The Bible tells about the new church. Peter and John were healing a lame man and preaching the Gospel of Christ when the priests and a captain put them in prison. However, there was no evidence to be found of any illegal activity on the part of Peter or John. Mistreatment of Christians became a usual occurrence."

"Why would someone not want people to change from their old, sinful ways to a new life in Christ?" you ask.

"Well, it's because the hearts of men are continually evil and the natural part of man cannot grasp the plan of God for us," I answer. "The Christian church grew despite the mistreatment of the disciples. It seems like the more the rulers tried to stamp out this Gospel way, the more attractive it became for many. In addition, the disciples performed miracles, which truly convinced many that there must be a power coming from above. Then deacons were chosen, and Stephen, being filled with the Holy Spirit, soon became a martyr, stoned to death for his faith. Then a very strange miracle happened. Saul, who had grown up a very strict Pharisee and who had consented to Stephen's stoning, was struck down by God. While Saul was traveling on the Damascus road, intending to persecute other Christians, God took the man's eyesight. In response, Saul repented of his evil intentions toward Christians, and he became a believer in Jesus. Saul actually became so humble that he accepted help from a Christian to restore his sight. On the road that day, Saul was renamed Paul by God. A persecutor of Christians became a Christian. God changed Saul's heart, and his life changed completely. The hunter becomes one of the hunted, and after many experiences with rulers, religious leaders, new Christians, and enemies, Paul, too, loses his life because of his Christian beliefs."

"This is another example for us," you say.

"Right! So right you are," I agree.

"What more do we need to know?" you ask.

"Let's finish reading through the Bible's New Testament

for our education. Then we'll kneel and pray until God saves our souls. Here, the Bible proves that it is for everyone. Peter was shown that God accepts not only Jews but also Gentiles. In fact, anyone who repents and forsakes their sins can have and know peace. Peter soon came to know Paul and realized that he must accept any and all people, even former persecutors, into the kingdom of God.

"Paul became the teacher of the new church, going from city to city, from church to church, traveling most of his Christian life, going into prison often, beaten with stripes and rods, stoned, shipwrecked three times, and abandoned for a night and a day in the deep. He was robbed, endured false brethren, and left in the wilderness, enduring pain, cold, nakedness, hunger, and thirst. In the midst of this, Paul said, 'I take pleasure in infirmities, in reproaches, in necessities, in persecutions, in distresses, for Christ's sake. For when I am weak, then am I strong; (2 Corinthians 12:10). Paul wrote many of the books of the Bible that we're reading. God inspired him, and he wrote by the leading of the Holy Spirit. We cannot take any of the Bible lightly. The reason that it agrees with itself and comes together as the law of God is because it was and is inspired by God.

"Are you having trouble with anything we have read and come to understand?" I ask.

"Why does it seem so hard to give in and change our lives?" you ask.

"It's because self—our desires—must die," I answer. "Like Jesus went to the cross and gave Himself, so we must take up our cross and give up our desires, deny ourselves and give up our wills in order to be His disciple. If you hadn't had the hell experience that we have had, could you commit yourself?"

"I don't know. I hope so. Others have, so there must be a way to take life seriously. There must be a way to catch the vision of eternity."

"The New Testament tells of the end of life, hell, and heaven. It tells us what we must do to go to each place, and it also tells us that there is no in-between place. The Bible tells us that God is gracious in giving us an option of escaping hell and more than gracious in giving us a chance to become God's son. The Bible tells us that we can be joint heirs with Jesus, God's Son, And that God himself, will be our Father. Does it seem to you that the New Testament is the road map to heaven? If so, the details are very important. If I follow a map but omit the small details, will I ever make it to my desired destination?"

"Oh, God, I will now kneel in prayer and make my commitment and ask for forgiveness of my sins. Please accept me!"

Scripture References for Chapter 7

1. Matthew 1
2. Matthew 2
3. Luke 2
4. Matthew 5, 6, 7
5. Mark 4:37–41
6. Matthew 8:28–34
7. Luke 15:11-32
8. John 6:9–14
9. Matthew 14:22–23
10. John 11:11–15
11. Matthew 4:1–11
12. Luke 5:4–9
13. Matthew 26
14. Mark 8:31–32
15. John 16:4–16
16. Revelation 22:12
17. John 5:26–29
18. Matthew 26:18–75
19. Matthew 27–28
20. Luke 24
21. Acts 2, 3, 4
22. Acts 10
23. Acts 7:55–60
24. Acts 9
25. 2 Corinthians 11:23–33
26. Mark 8:34–38
27. Luke 9:23–24
28. Matthew 25:29–46
29. 2 Peter 3:9–12
30. Romans 8:16–18

Chapter 8
Repenting and Coming to God

"TELL ME! TELL ME your experience. How did God accept and forgive you?" I ask.

"Well first, let me say that there is nothing in this world that feels as good as this." "There is no pleasure I've ever had, no experience I've ever gone through, and nothing I can compare to the feeling of forgiveness for my sins. I realize by now that feelings are not the only gauge to go by. Faith and acceptance are a very big part of forgiveness, because God can only accept those who believe in Him and trust Him. When we were going through our experience of hell and I realized that I was not a child of God, I became very serious about the fact that life was not supposed to be selfishly all about me. Our short study of the Old and New Testament has helped me to understand what God wants from me. My picture of life has changed dramatically. Life isn't supposed to be about me, except for my decision about salvation. Yes, I need to be concerned first about my personal salvation, but when all is well between God and me, my thoughts should be about others.

"The act of conversion is a very simple step. The giving up of 'self' is difficult, but when I got past that, conversion was not complicated. Jesus said His yoke is easy and His burden is light. Faith or acceptance of biblical truth and God's spirit speaking to us brings us to a change in attitude, and our willingness to obey God's spirit and His Word and our faithfulness in all things keeps us on the road to heaven. We want to be with other believers."

"This is what happened. I knelt down and told God, 'I am tired of my sinful life, and, God, after going through this hell experience, I know it's not an option, Lord, to take a chance with being careless. I have decided to follow Jesus all the way. Whatever it takes to be saved is easily worth it. Like the Apostle Paul, who changed his life completely, I will change too. If you, God, will forgive my sins and give me peace in my heart, I promise to serve you and be faithful to you all my life. I will obey, and when I fail, I will keep my heart contrite and broken so repentance and confession will be a part of my life. I want to be humble, and, Lord, if and when pride takes hold of me, help me to deal with it very quickly. Helping others in any way is my desire, especially if I can help them come to you. I will serve you all my life. Amen.'"

"Well, I just want you to know that your experience seems very good to me, and I believe God has accepted you as His child," I say. "Though your life will have ups and downs, God has promised that He will not let us be tempted beyond what we are able to bear."

"The experience God gave me is very special," I say, "and I hope to treasure it all my days. I have felt bad for a long, long time, and I thank God for not bringing the world into judgment and for sparing my life until this time. To somehow catch the vision of eternity and hell and determine within myself that I cannot go there remains a highlight of my life.

"With tears running down my cheeks and a burden on my heart for my sinful life, as the Lord was speaking to me, a song was sung in church about coming to earth's borderland, and the night when I made my decision to follow God, my choice touched me because I realized that I didn't have what it took to be saved. I knew that I couldn't do it alone, and God gave me the grace to walk to the front of the church and ask for prayers when the ministers gave me the opportunity. A softness came over me that hadn't been there for a long time. The willingness to make a change became very important to me, and then God took over. It seemed like He did most of the rest. The next morning, my family and I were going on a small vacation for a day or two. God stayed with me, and He began to show me my life as He saw it. Mostly, He showed me the areas of my life where I had been wrong. Because I had lived for a long time in sin, after leaving God years before, there was much for Him to show me, many areas where 'self' had done as it had pleased. As we traveled, it seemed as if my heart softened more and more. As we ate lunch, tears began running down my cheeks. My family wondered, 'What's wrong with Dad? Why is he crying?' There wasn't any way to stop the tears, so they flowed and flowed. During this time, God was melting my heart more and more. Surrender was happening, and giving up 'self' was feeling better and better. After lunch, we boarded a boat to visit an island, and while I was sitting in the back of the boat, tears still running down my cheeks, God told me, 'You are saved!' Yes, the thought came flooding over me that if this boat sinks, all is well, and I am saved, and heaven is my home. The tears of sorrow, the commitment I had made, and the confessions I had made to Him all came together to become tears of rejoicing. I felt so complete and accepted by God that nothing has ever come close to this overwhelming feeling.

"I was very encouraged when I shared with my minister what God had done for me. Then I was able to share my experience with the church, and everyone believed that God had forgiven me. It was so wonderful to know that all was well.

"God had given me what my heart had longed for, but He still had several confessions and actions that He wanted me to take. I found that with God's help, I was able to do everything he wanted me to do. As I obeyed Him, each of my actions came with a feeling of peace. However, even before we got home from our vacation, God tested me. Would I obey Him? It seemed like a small thing God asked me to do, and maybe I could have excused it; however, if obedience to God is not important in the small things, then lack of obedience becomes a joy stealer and finally will take you down.

"One day in a grocery store, it seemed as if God was asking me to make a confession to a man I had previously worked with. This confession was not easy, but it was very rewarding when I was able to obey.

"However, an even greater experience occurred. God brought all of the details together. One day, a man with whom I'd had little contact drove up my driveway. Before my repentance experience, I had visited a place with this man, a place that I knew I shouldn't have gone to. After my experience, I knew that I should talk to him, but I didn't know how because he lived some distance from my house. However, God knew how. As the man was passing near my house that day, some other men told him where I lived. I just happened to be home, working on a remodeling project with my son, when he drove up my driveway. The instant I saw this man, I knew that God was working out the details so I could speak with him. Of course, the devil entered the picture as well, telling me that I didn't need to say anything. But a little voice said, 'Now's your time.' With God's help, I was able to lay my heart open with this man. It seems amazing how God works out the details for us when we are His willing servants.

"God has asked me to do many things for Him. Some seemed difficult, and with no praise coming from men, but I have found that willingness counts much with God. He will reward us as He sees fit, and if not now, then He will do so in eternity. The Bible says we need to be clay in the potter's hands. That must mean not to fight Him or want our own way but just to let Him have His way with me..

"Now that all is well, my experience with hell sometimes starts to seem like a distant memory, and life goes on. Day by day, night by night, time is passing. 'Oh, God, help me not to forget that terrible experience of feeling lost,' I say. 'I know I need the keenness of it to help keep me on the narrow way. You, God, never intended for people to go to hell. You made hell for the devil and his angels. Sin can't go to heaven, and unrepentant people have sin in their lives. The Bible, your Word, doesn't have another place. So then, if sin can't go to heaven, whoever is living in sin at the end of their lives must go to hell! You are a jealous God, and you have the right to be. Those who reject your Son, who died for the sins of everyone, will be judged and lost forever.'

"To some, this may seem hard. The world offers many things, and to be children of God, we must turn down many things. We must give up many pleasures of the world. There are many places we cannot go, many things we cannot do. We must live on a higher plain, one way above the lust and pride of the world. If this seems difficult, then return to the beginning of this book and think about hell again. Would a little pleasure be worth a hundred years like that ... or a thousand years like that ... or a million years like that, or how about unending doom forever? We decided—you and me—that we'll give up a little to gain a lot. This is far above winning the lottery or being born into the richest family in the world, because the world will be destroyed."

Scripture References for Chapter 8

1. Hebrews 11:6
2. Luke 10:27–28
3. Isaiah 35:8
4. Matthew 10:39
5. Matthew 11:29–30
6. Matthew 3:8
7. Luke 24:47
8. Acts 26:20
9. Romans 2:4
10. 2 Corinthians 7:9–10
11. Acts 5:29
12. Romans 6:12–16
13. Hebrews 10:25
14. Psalms 34:18
15. 1 Corinthians 10:13
16. Matthew 5:12
17. Colossians 3:23–25
18. Revelation 22:12
19. Isaiah 64:8
20. Matthew 25:41
21. Revelation 21:27
22. Exodus 20: 5
23. Revelation 21:7–8
24. Luke 14:33
25. Colossians 3:1–2
26. Titus 2:12
27. 1 Peter 2:11
28. Romans 13:14
29. 1 John 2:15–16
30. Revelation 20: 10-15
31. 2 Peter 3:7–12

CHAPTER 9
LIVING ON THE HIGHER PLAIN

"**N**OW COMES THE WALK, Many have come to God and found a release. They have had their burdens lifted and have come to some peace with themselves. Some have made a connection with God but have soon drifted back to the desires of their flesh. We need a greater plan that will carry us all the way to heaven."

"Yes, you are very right," you say. "Please explain this to me."

"The answer is called the grace of God—living in the grace of God. When we are completely His, we live in God's favor. Our unintentional sins are covered by Jesus's atoning blood, which He shed for us. Our sins are not imputed to us, and we remain as though we have no sin. In order to keep this blessed state, we must be obedient to God, His Holy Spirit, His church, and sometimes others' direction. This walk denies our desires often, and the real question becomes this: 'What does God want me to do?' Jesus said we were bought with a price and we are not our own. The theme of our lives becomes obedience to Jesus, and even this life has rewards far beyond selfish living."

"Do you think a life of obedience is possible?" you ask. "Is God really asking this much?"

"Yes. It's going to take faith, a faith that sees beyond earthly life. Remember, you aren't living this way just for the present, and though you will have struggles and trials, you will fall short of the mark many times. The devil will even tell us, 'There's no use. Others can live for God, but you can't.' Here's where we'll need a strong and honest faith. When we've done our best and acknowledged our failures, confessing our sins, we must accept in faith and believe. Having faith means believing the Word of God. Faith grasps the promises of God. Faith makes it possible to see the present and the future, and if I have faith, I believe that nothing is impossible for God. The true believer's faith will bring him or her through this life and save him or her for the next life. The true believer believes the Bible as it is written, even where it is not understood or cannot be proven. There are many examples in the Bible where faith worked, and it will work for us as well.

"God's Word says without faith, it is impossible to please God. Abraham believed God, even when God's words to him looked unreasonable and hopeless. When Abraham obeyed, God worked miracles to honor His Word and make Abraham a great nation. He said, 'And in thy seed shall all the nations of the earth be blessed, because thou hast obeyed my voice' (Genesis 23:18). We must have a living faith, a faith that sees God's plan and what it will do for us. Faith has the power to carry us through this life successfully."

"That's a tall order, my friend," you say. "Tell me more."

"Yes, okay," I continue. "We have hardly started explaining

the true Christian life. The emphasis is on 'life.' A true Christian must be alive. In order to live, one must take in food. Jesus said that spiritual food is much different than natural food; however, it also keeps life going. Jesus is the Word, and the Bible is either describing His words or pointing to or after His words. Obedience to Jesus is the plan of salvation. Without Him, the Bible would be void and useless. Reading, meditation, and listening are ways of feeding our spiritual nature. The Bible must become precious to us. We cannot go from day to day thinking we have all the answers and believing that we are able to remain committed on our own strength. We must search and pray and have open minds to listen. Do you remember the Holy Spirit? It is that little voice, that impression that comes to you. It is God! He's speaking. Listen to Him. The Holy Spirit has promised to lead us and guide us into all truth. Listen to God's voice often. The more you give yourself to Him in obedience, the more He will communicate with you."

"Now I can see. Indeed, the Christian life will take much effort to live. It is not just a decision and then the status quo. There really must be a changed life. But what about forgiveness?" you ask. "God forgave you, so how will you forgive others?"

"Let's say someone just committed a horrible wrong against you and you have every earthly reason to not forgive them. In fact, you want to say bad things about them and harm them if you can. The devil tells you to get even, to fight back, to teach them a lesson. The little voice comes to you and says, 'Forgive them.' You just read in the Bible last night that you must forgive them if you are to be forgiven by God. What are you going to do? Many thoughts flash through your mind. Hurts from the past present themselves, and the battle is real. Now's the time to pray and tell God about it. He understands you, and He will give you the ability to forgive … if you are willing. When you remember how Jesus forgave you, you must always forgive others. This may be one of your hardest tests and one of the most rewarding when completed."

"I can tell you now, I will need help," you say. "It will take more than my abilities to live this Christian life. It will take a higher power. I will need to lean on God's everlasting arms and on others to help me."

"Let's talk about love," I say. "Everyone wants to be loved and to share their love with someone. Now our first love must be to God. We must love Him more than anyone or anything. The first commandment in the Bible says, Thou shalt love the Lord thy God with all thy heart, soul, mind, and strength; (Mark 12:30). This becomes the reason why we obey God. We obey because we love Him and our relationship with Him is more precious than any other. Every relationship on earth is second to the commitment we made to God. The reason for this first love is that God loved us so much that He gave His only begotten Son, Jesus, to die for our sins so that we could be saved. Never has there been a love like this. Our second love, one to others, has also changed. We see others as souls God created, and our love reaches out to them. We want to do something to help them turn to God and save their souls. This becomes our desire, and we love everyone.

"Love to our families has also changed. Instead of carnal love that pleases only the flesh, our love becomes complete and puts our actions into their proper perspective. Our desire wants to put our families and others before ourselves. This is true love, and it takes a power from God to be able to live it."

"Wow!" you exclaim. "I didn't know that someone could

change so much. This is indeed a different life. Could you tell me about the 'other cheek?' Didn't Jesus say that if people smite you on one cheek to offer your other cheek so they may hit you there as well?"

"Yes!" I say. "We call this nonresistance. It means that you don't fight back, that you don't take someone to court. For some in the past as well as now, it means dying for their faith. Because they believe in Jesus and won't give up their relationship with Him, they become like Jesus, like a lamb. Jesus even healed the soldier's ear when His disciple cut it off. Jesus healed the very one who tried to harm Him. The Christian is called to do good in response to evil."

"I suppose you can see the gears in my head turning very quickly," you say. "Come on! Am I really supposed to think this way?"

"Thoughts!" I say. "Someone once said, 'What you think is what you are.'"

"Many problems and the things we are talking about start with thoughts," I say. "On this higher plain of living, your thoughts must be controlled. Evil thoughts lead to all kinds of sins. Jesus made thoughts equal with deeds in our hearts. He said that if you hate someone, you are a murderer. If you have lustful thoughts, you are committing adultery. Thoughts can cross our minds instantly, and we are not held accountable for passing thoughts. When we let thoughts dwell in our minds, they become unacceptable and must be dealt with. If evil thoughts come to you, go and pray and read the Bible and ask God to take them away. If you dwell on bad thoughts about others or lust or deeds, you will be separating yourself from God. Only He knows how long you are in His grace with this behavior."

"It will take a power I don't have, so God must help me, and I know He will," you say. "Please go on. What's next?"

"We need to talk about honesty," I say. "Every Christian must be honest. Telling lies, deceiving, and changing the truth are not of God but from the devil. He was a liar from the beginning and the father of lies. To intentionally lie is a sin that must be repented of. God is all about truth. Jesus called Himself the way, the truth, and the life. The Christian life is about truth, and lies have ruined many a person. How can you love someone if you lie to him or her? Our tongues can be our worst enemies. It does us so much good when they are used properly and so much evil when they are used improperly. It is such a little member of our body, and yet the Bible compares it to a small rudder that can move the whole ship. We must guard our tongue and keep it for God's use. Then it can be a very special member to help others and ourselves."

"Thank you for those statements," you say. "Lord, please help me to never tell another lie and to keep my tongue pure."

"The next subject is works," I continue. "Not work, but works—the things I do for God. These are not things I do to earn my salvation. No, salvation is a free gift that we receive when we meet the conditions of a broken spirit and a contrite heart, repenting of our sins. Works are the things I do for God because I love Him. I want to be part of His kingdom and useful. So I pray for others and help others in many ways by giving my time, talents, and money to help them. Naturally and spiritually, I want to be a worker for you, Lord. So what do you have for me to do? These works must be done with humility, not pride, not for show, not for honor to my name, and not letting my right hand know what my left hand is doing, so to speak. In this Christian living on a higher plain, God receives all of the honor, and I am just a servant doing my duty."

"You mention humility," you say. "Please tell me more about humility."

"Do you think you are humble, dear one? It has been said that if you think you're humble, you're probably not." Many Christians have trouble in their lives because of pride and the attitudes and spirits they allow that come from a proud heart. Humility may be one of the hardest attributes to keep in place, and it will take God's help to keep ourselves in our proper place. We want to judge ourselves by our intentions and compare ourselves to others. Then we come up with a picture that is totally incorrect. If we can look at ourselves through the eyes of God, then we will realize the deceitfulness and wickedness of our hearts because we are only sinners saved by grace. Then surely, pride will leave, and by God's grace, we can be humble Christians. Humble Christians are the only ones God really can use. Pride has its own agenda and is useless in God's kingdom."

"What about church? Do I need to go to church, or can I just be a Christian and keep all of this between God and me?"

"While you don't have to have a church to be saved, there are many things written in the Bible that cannot be practiced unless you go to church and unless you go to a church that practices all of the commandments of God," I say. "Baptism, discipline, unity, feet-washing, the Lord's Supper, the holy kiss, and reproof are some biblical practices that must take place in a community setting. God commands that Christians practice these beliefs in church. Then there is preaching the Word, Sunday school, midweek meeting, singing, and fellowship, all of which is very encouraging for the practicing Christian. If we attempt to live our lives on our own without the accountability of fellow believers, how would we know if a strange spirit was overtaking us? We might even lose our way. The Bible says we are to be our brother's keeper. We all need help. None is an island to himself, and nobody has all of the right answers. Baptism is an outward sign of an inward cleansing, and it is the door into the church. Baptism alone doesn't save anyone; however, it shows our willingness to be part of the organized church, and we make promises to be faithful and do our part in keeping the church pure and cleansed from sin. Discipline has always been part of God's law, and who can administer it except the church? Unity is necessary, the Bible says, because how can two walk together unless they agree? We must have the same goals and purposes in life because, aren't we traveling the same road and planning to reach the same destination? Feet-washing is a humble act that Jesus practiced on his disciples and commanded us to do. Jesus told Peter that if He didn't wash Peter's feet, then Peter would have no part with Him. Did Jesus mean that only for one time? If so, then this teaching is different from His other teachings. The Lord's Supper or Communion is commanded and is a very serious act. Jesus said to examine yourself to make sure your life is what it is supposed to be, and if we eat the bread and drink the cup unworthily, we are guilty of His death. The holy kiss is almost nonexistent and practiced by few, yet it is commanded by Paul and others. It shows the close connection of the brotherhood, and it reveals that fact that there must be love for each other to practice these commands. Reproof is another command of the Bible. When I am a humble Christian, I believe it is my brother's business to help prove my life, and if he sees that I may be taking the wrong way in some part of my life, he should talk to me about it. He doesn't come in a condescending way but in a humble way, realizing that he also has or could have some struggles in this area. This is truly helping each other.

"The preaching of the Word must be directed by God, and it is a very effective way for God to guide our lives. Many times, Christians have seen areas of their lives where God would want a cleansing, a new commitment, or some change that draws them closer to Him. Sunday school has helped so much. Sharing and listening to thoughts and struggles of others becomes an encouragement to us many times. Knowing that we all have the same struggles and tendencies gives us the courage to continue on the narrow way of life. Midweek meetings are a great encouragement and are like a drink of water to a thirsty soul halfway between a weekly meal. We need all of the advantages we can receive because the devil will use every opportunity to trip us and make our lives miserable. Singing a song in praise to God or listening to one about heaven can be very comforting, and sometimes a song can reprove. Sometimes it makes us feel good, and sometimes it makes us feel bad. Songs move us! Happy hearts have a song to sing, and nobody can take away a song. Beautiful singing seems to draw us to God. As the birds praise Him in song, so should we. A song in our hearts is a touch of heaven here below. Sing often and praise Him more. Fellowship encourages us. We were never meant to be alone. Even Jesus, who was God on earth and complete because He needed nothing, had those who were very close to Him, and He wanted them by His side. He wanted their fellowship, and we all need connections with others. Christian fellowship makes the narrow way seem a little wider. It makes God seem a little closer. It makes the devil seem a little weaker, and it makes heaven seem more real."

"I am impressed!" you say. "Now I see the higher plain. It

seems to be above the ground, a little higher path. The temptations could be fewer because you explained a way of living that's like being on a bridge above most of the people and the evil things below. In a sense, we're disconnected from the world and living our lives between earth and heaven, and as we stay on this higher plain, we have the foretaste of heaven here below."

"Yes," I admit, "you have the vision, although at best, as the Bible say, we see through a glass only darkly. Then our faith increases our vision. The goal is like a shining city in the distance. We want to arrive there. As the years go by, the city becomes brighter and brighter. Earth and its ways seem less and less important. Our journey is almost over, and like the song says, deliverance will come. And finally, deliverance has come!"

Scripture References for Chapter 9

1. Luke 9:23
2. Luke 9:62
3. Romans 4:24–25
4. Romans 5:16–21
5. Hebrews 5:9
6. Acts 5:29–32
7. Romans 6:12–18
8. 1 Corinthians 6:19–20
9. Hebrews 11
10. Romans 14:8
11. John 14:19
12. 2 Timothy 2: 15
13. John 10
14. Psalms 19:7–14
15. 1 Peter 1
16. Psalms 119:105
17. Hebrews 5:6–7
18. Matthew 18:4
19. 2 Corinthians 12:9
20. 1 Kings 19:11–13
21. John 14:15–26
22. John 15:26–27
23. John 16:7–13
24. Matthew 6:12–15
25. Luke 23:34
26. Deuteronomy 33:27
27. James 5:16
28. Matthew 18:15–16
29. Matthew 23:37–40
30. Matthew 28:19
31. Philippians 2:4
32. 2 Corinthians 5:17
33. Luke 6:29
34. Acts 8:32

35. Luke 22:49–51
36. Romans 12:14–21
37. Proverbs 23:7
38. 1 John 3:14–18
39. Luke 8:15
40. 2 Corinthians 13:7
41. Philippians 4:8
42. 1 Peter 2:12
43. John 14:6
44. James 1:26
45. James 3:5–18
46. James 2:14–26
47. Romans 5:15–19
48. Psalms 34:18
49. Matthew 3:2
50. Mark 1:15
51. Luke 13:3–5
52. Acts 2:38
53. 2 Chronicles 7:14
54. 1 Peter 5:6
55. 1 John 2:16
56. James 4:6
57. Proverbs 6:17
58. Romans 9:20–24
59. Luke 17:10
60. 2 Corinthians 10:12–18
61. Hebrews 10:23–25
62. Acts 2:38
63. Galatians 6:1–2
64. Matthew 18:17
65. Psalms 133:1
66. Ephesians 4:2–6
67. John 13:3–10
68. Matthew 26:26–30
69. 1 Corinthians 16:20
70. 2 Corinthians 13:12

71. 2 Timothy 4:2
72. Ephesians 5:10–13
73. 2 Timothy 4:2
74. 1 John 1:7
75. Genesis 4:9
76. 1 Timothy 4:1
77. 1 Corinthians 10:13
78. John 17:10–23
79. 1 Corinthians 13:12
80. Revelation 21:10–27

CHAPTER 10
HEAVEN: THE LAND OF PURE DELIGHT

"**T**HERE WON'T BE ANY pain, tears, fears, cancer, strokes, aches, annoyances, anxieties, or diseases of any kind," I say. "No anger, misuses, force, degradation, spite, backbiting, backstabbing, offense, murder, rape, or mistreatment. No more taxes, bills to pay, rent due, remodeling, overhauling, fixing, building, tearing down, maintenance, or plumbing. There won't be any waste, recycling, disposing of, getting rid of, downsizing, or trash of any kind. It won't be too hot, too cold, too wet, too dry, foggy, cloudy, or too humid. There won't be storms, earthquakes, tornadoes, hurricanes, thunder, lightning, winds, floods, or forest fires. Things will not wear out, rust, fall apart, corrode, leak, or deteriorate in any way. We won't need money, food, drink, soap, towels, degreasers, or cleaning supplies of any kind. There will be no use for gas, oil, propane, coal, nuclear power, or solar power. Wars, fighting, bombs, guns, and all such equipment will be missing. Use of cars, trucks, airplanes, trains, and transportation vehicles will be nonexistent. There is no night here. This land is completely different. Have you ever experienced perfection?"

"No, and this is scary!" you say. "How will we act? What will we do? Where will we go? Will God be beside me all the time? Will Jesus see me then?"

"Stop! You have earthly thoughts, and earth is not here in heaven," I say. "Most likely, in the past, you wondered what we will do in heaven. Maybe you even thought you might become bored, or you wondered what we will do all of the time, especially without night and living forever. First, we must realize that we will have a different body, a spiritual one, a body not limited by time or space. Miles will mean nothing. Getting here or there will be instantaneous. Things that limit us on earth have changed, and a great gulf may be our only limit, as God said a great gulf will be fixed and we will not cross it. Nor would we want to. Hell is on the other side, and no one in heaven will ever see that place."

"Our bodies will be changed in the twinkling of an eye, the Bible says. Do you think we'll still be male and female?" you ask "Will I know you, and will you know me?"

"The Bible says we'll be known as we are known. I believe we'll recognize each other and we'll know our loved ones. We'll know all of the Bible characters, and we'll know everyone there. Part of knowing us as we are known includes that nothing is hidden from us. 'God, our father—we, His sons—joint heirs with Jesus; (Romans 8:17). We'll be spiritual beings, have much more understanding, and be much more alive than we are now. Notice – (God's sons.) It is likely that male and female were only for our earthly life. There will be no gender in heaven. We also think of handicapped people on earth, whether physical or mental. They will shed all of their disabilities in heaven. Sin will not exist, and because sin was the reason for our frailties, heaven will hold perfect beings."

"How about the angels?" you ask. "What is their role? How will we relate to them?"

"Could it be that they are God's workers?" I say. "It appears that at the last day, God will bring angels to help with the judging of the people on the earth. The Bible says that Michael, the archangel, shall stand with one foot on land and one foot on sea and declare that time shall be no more. The Bible says that God will bring his holy angels with Him to judge the world. The Bible also tells us that Jesus was going back to heaven and that He would prepare mansions for all those who love and serve Him. It would seem that angels surely are involved in preparing these mansions, whatever these words mean. I don't believe this means 'houses' or that the mansions are individual places. I think that mansions are being prepared for everyone. Heaven will be a very big place. There will be many places for us to go, much to see, and pleasures in heaven will be many times greater than what we have ever experienced. We who have been redeemed will have a special place in God's heart because we made use of His plan and did not allow Jesus to waste His sacrifice for us. We allowed Jesus's blood to be applied to our lives, and we gave up 'self' for Him. Though man was made a little lower than the angels, according to the Bible, by being saved, man becomes a saint. We had a high calling. We accepted the call, and God accepted us. We will be unable to measure how blessed we will be!

"Our relationship with the angels will be very interesting. The angels may wonder at times how this came about and what it was like to feel lost. What did condemnation feel like? Because we experienced a life that angels have never lived and we made it to heaven, angels may use us in a special way. I believe that we will love angels exceedingly because they have been God's ministering servants."

"Will God have a throne?" you ask. "Will he be like a king? And what about Jesus? Will He be near us and with us?"

"God will not and has never been like the kings we've known on earth," I answer. "God is love, and His love will be increased in heaven. The Bible tells us that we'll see Him face-to-face—face-to-face with Jesus and face-to-face with God! The love will flow. We'll never feel slighted or jealous, and we'll never feel as if God or Jesus loves someone more than us. Remember, these sins don't exist in heaven. All is peaceful. We will never even have a bad thought. Can you imagine that? The Bible says that He will wipe all tears from our eyes. Never before will we have felt love like this love."

"You are making me lonesome. I feel like I'm ready to go. The love is drawing me like I have never felt before."

"Bless you," I say. "It's very good for a Christian to have these feelings at times, and though we want to live on earth and enjoy our time here, we have a longing for that better land. The soul God gave us longs to return back to Him. The Bible says to set our affections on things above, not on things on the earth. It says that we should have these earthly things as though we have them not and that we should be pilgrims and strangers on the earth. When we became converted, our real home became heaven. Our time on earth is so short, it hardly counts for a home."

"I heard a song about hills in glory land," you mention to me. "What do you think? Will we stroll through the hills and valleys of heaven?"

"Yes, likely so," I say. "When God created the earth, He

made the beautiful Garden of Eden. Maybe that garden or one like it will be in heaven. The tree of life, the river, the trees that bear their fruit will all be there. The garden should be next to the city with its golden streets. Precious stones are all around, making up the foundation of the wall and gates of pearl shining in every direction. Just outside the gardens are the hills of glory. They go on and on. They are full of mystical happenings and objects—things that are pleasing to the eyes and ears and touch. It is plain to see. We'll spend much of eternity exploring wonders like we have never seen. Every move will be so effortless, and our being will never tire. It would seem that everything in heaven will be in perfect order. We will have our worship time, singing and praising God and the lamb, Jesus. We'll be singing in perfect harmony without mistakes, no off-key notes, no discords, and every song in perfect timing. The Bible says we'll experience pleasures forevermore."

"What about children?" you ask. "Where are they? What will they do, and how will they act? Will we know the difference?"

"Oh, children! All of them are in heaven. Everyone who hadn't come to the age of being accountable comes to heaven. Jesus loved little children. There are more children in heaven than any other age by far. Their role is a great one. Though they never became converted, their sins were covered by Jesus's sacrifice, and because of their innocence, they are saved. Maybe the angels will take care of them. It would seem that because sin isn't in heaven and all is perfection, the care of children would take care of itself in many ways. Can you see Jesus in the midst of multitudes of children? Some are on His lap. Some are in His arms, and they are all getting along and waiting their turn to receive a hug from Him. This scene will repeat over and over again. The children will see the scars on His hands and feet. They will wonder, *Why?* Jesus will tell them, and they will understand. The love He gave will bless them."

"That statement brings a question to my mind," you say. "What will we say about the hands and feet of our Savior?"

"The redeemed will have a special feeling about those hands and feet," I assert. "The scars will appear as the most beautiful sight. The scars mean that we, the redeemed, can be in heaven. The scars prove Jesus's sacrifice for our sins. Without the scars, we wouldn't have made it. Without the scars, God's plan wouldn't have been complete. Jesus is not embarrassed about His hands and feet. He knows the cost was great, and He knows the cost was worth it all. God and Jesus made the plan so we could be in heaven."

"Rest, sleep, naps—these gave us a great feeling on earth. Will we rest or sleep in heaven?" you ask.

"Sometimes we say we will rest from our labors in heaven. We talk about resting and the land of rest. However, sleep, most likely, is not a part of heaven. The Bible says there will be no night there. We never think of God or Jesus sleeping in heaven. Our changed bodies will not need sleep. The heavenly rest of the soul is a blissful condition, and we will always be comfortable, never aware of any lack, never experiencing uneasy feelings, never encountering anything that causes us to fear or tremble. The home of the soul will seem like the place we really ought to be."

"So then, what do you think of temptations?" you then ask. "On earth, we had so many temptations. It was like I couldn't go anywhere or do anything or even just be awake without temptations always before me. The devil made sure of that."

"That will be the victory of all victories!" I exclaim. "There will be no temptation—never a bad thought or deed. We won't have to worry at all that someone around us will lie or cheat or kill or steal. Nobody will ever treat us badly. Neither we nor they will ever be offended or greedy or gossiping or misunderstood. There will be no covetousness or temptations of any kind. The devil and his angels who brought the temptation will be in hell. Their power to deceive and tempt will be over. Jesus will have locked them in the depths of the bottomless pit, never to tempt or destroy again. Now we can be free to do and to live righteously. This will be like the day God took our sins away, and it will keep going forever."

"After the resurrection, Jesus was able to be a spirit or a person in body," you say. "Will it be like that for us? He moved or appeared at will. Buildings didn't hold Him out. Nothing could stop Him from going where He desired. Do you think heaven will be like that for us?"

"I believe it will!" I explain. "Time will mean nothing. Miles will mean nothing. Sometimes we see pictures of angels with wings. The Book of Revelation in the Bible speaks of their wings. This could mean an overshadowing power. Jesus used a comparison in the Book of Matthew of a hen gathering her chicks under her wings. However, our new body and spirit won't need wings to fly, but just as God and Jesus and the Holy Spirit move now, so will we. In heaven, we will be much more alive than now. We will be so much more alert. Our attention will be focused, and we'll miss nothing. In earthly terms, we could be a thousand miles away but still know exactly what's going on in the city of golden streets. Then, if need be, we could be there in a moment. Past limits don't hold us anymore. Heaven doesn't have gravity pulling us down. We can be in the air or on a hard surface without effort. We used to think that flying at a thousand miles per hour would be super fast. Now we move that quickly just by desiring to be there."

"Will our voices all sound the same?" you then ask. "Will everyone understand each other? Can we speak to the men of the Bible? Will they tell us stories like we used to read? How much will we talk about our past, our life on earth?"

"Oh, these are good questions. I believe we will. Let's begin with Adam and Eve. Can you imagine asking them about their life before sin, about walking with God in the cool of the day? Would Adam talk about that terrible day when they took the forbidden fruit and spiritually died? Or will heaven be too sacred to talk about sin? Adam could tell us about naming the animals and then how God made a helpmeet for him. Think of it! Adam was alone, and then God created Eve. And then he had someone to share his life with, one who could communicate with him, one who loved him so much more than the animals could, and one who would bear children for them. Oh, if they just wouldn't have sinned, and the world could have remained perfect. But then we wouldn't have the opportunity to go to heaven. God's plan was great, and we won't blame Adam.

"Imagine talking to Noah. He would tell us about preaching for 120 years, telling people what God had said. How did he live with himself knowing that all those people would be destroyed and then to see and hear that nobody cared or believed him? After he built the ark as God commanded, when the animals began coming on board, how must he have felt, knowing the power of God to turn the animals against their natures? If people had been unbelievers before, how could they remain so, watching wild animals walking in twos into this building made by man? How could they not believe Noah's preaching? It seems that something would have registered in their hearts, something telling that God was serious. Then the rains came down, and the souls drowned one by one. Noah had to begin life after the flood with just his family. I believe he will tell us his experiences. Surely, they must have been unique.

"How about sitting down with Abraham and hearing all the details of his dealings with God? He didn't know what to expect. One day, he had his promised son, and shortly thereafter, God told him to sacrifice that precious son on an altar. Was it hard to obey? Abraham, the father of faith—oh, how he trusted God. Then we need to talk about Lot and his problems—Lot's grace in fleeing the city while his wife disobeyed and became a pillar of salt.

"We will hear from Moses. He was saved by God in an unusual way. The Egyptian king's daughter wanted baby Moses for her own child. However, she had Moses's mother care for the infant. All of this was part of God's plan. After he grew up, Moses chose to suffer with his Jewish culture, God's chosen people, rather than live in the king's palace. He was chosen by God to lead the children of Israel. Can you hear Moses telling us about the plan, the plagues, the departure, and then being pursued by the king's army? Can you hear him telling of the miracle at the Red Sea, the water parting and standing up like a wall, the ground underneath dry? Imagine Moses describing the Israelites crossing the dry riverbed and then watching the king's army caught as the wall of water returns. God's people are free. However, it seems as if their trouble is just beginning. I believe Moses will be able to tell us many more things than we read in the Bible. He will be a most interesting companion.

"Then we'll meet Joseph, the dreamer. Who gave him his

dreams? God had quite a plan. Several times, it looked like Joseph was doomed, but each time, God brought His will to pass. Just think of being in heaven, sitting with Joseph, and listening to him tell us the story of his life. To hear what Joseph was feeling as his brothers betrayed him, and when he had the chance to get even with them, with tears in his eyes, he forgave them. What a powerful story of God's grace. God was surely with this man, and it will be a joy to hear his story.

"To sit with David, the man after God's own heart, will be a great honor. As a boy, David delivered the sheep from the bear and the lion. He was the only man brave enough to fight and kill Goliath. God was on David's side, and David knew that. He trusted God, and most of the time, he seemed to do as God directed. When he disobeyed, David had a repentant spirit. When he was told about his sins, David repented. It will be a pleasure to talk to David, the shepherd boy who became a king and the writer of most of the Psalms. It seems that David praised God more than anyone we know, and surely, it will be the same way in heaven. I hope to hear the stories from David firsthand.

"There was a biblical man, Job. He struggled repeatedly because the devil was trying to prove to God that Job only served God because God took care of Job and gave him great abundance. We know the story, having read it many times. We've admired Job's determination and faithfulness. How small do you think his struggles will seem to him in heaven? I suppose that Job will be reluctant to talk about his struggles and loss, yet, as we know, no one can make the events more real than the person who was there. Let's spend a while with Job.

"Imagine walking with Daniel in the hills of glory as he shares his past life. Could he tell us how he really felt in the lion's den? Would he say what his thoughts were regarded those who wanted to harm him? How did he feel when the king came and asked him if his God, whom he served, had delivered him from the hungry lions? Daniel would probably want to know how we got converted and how our lives changed when Jesus came into our hearts. Maybe Daniel would wonder what it was like to have the whole Bible available to read.

"I surely want to listen to Shadrach, Meshach, and Abednego as they explain what it was like to be in the terrible furnace when someone joined them and saved them. What determination they had! They were a very good example for us, teaching us to obey God. Surely, it will be a pleasure to be with them and hear the details of their stories. It is a relief to know that nothing like this will ever happen again. In heaven, we'll have no enemies.

"We'll talk to Elijah and Elisha. These prophets of God had direction. They knew when God was speaking. It will be wonderful to walk and talk with them, to hear their wisdom. I am sure they are so glad to be in heaven. The hard messages they brought from God to men are now over, and all they know is peace and joy forever.

"Think of Samson. What a man he was! Just think of what he could have accomplished if his energy would have been directed entirely toward God's purpose. Surely, the strongest man who ever lived will have interesting stories. Will there be feelings of regret in heaven, or will all negative thoughts be left behind? We don't know what Samson will have to say. The Bible appears to list him among the faithful, so I believe his changed heart will speak of how good God was to him.

"Remember that all those who lived in the time before Jesus will also ask us many questions. How did we become so blessed?

We had the opportunity to become born again, to become a new creature in Christ, to have the Holy Spirit of God to lead us and guide us into all truth. We are redeemed by the blood of the lamb. Their only way to heaven was by looking forward and following God's commandments. It will surely look to them like we have been given a more glorious way to be saved."

"Tell me the reason why we are here," you ask in excitement.

"It's Jesus!" I exclaim. "Without Him, no man would be saved." Most of our thoughts will be about the one who redeemed us and His Father, who allowed our salvation. Their love brought us here, and nothing in heaven can be more appealing than the Father and the Son. Our praises will ring throughout eternity for them. The nail scars in Jesus's hands and feet will always remind us of the cost. Though we will love each other and will have many conversations and precious experiences, none will come close to our Savior and God.

"It is easy to understand why we will want to have many conversations with Paul. He had so many experiences. We read of his conversion in Acts Chapter 9. Surely, he will tell us of his willingness to change his mind, though he was a strong-willed man. God chose to penetrate his heart and mind, and Saul, who persecuted Christians and consented to their deaths, became Paul, a Christ-following leader of Christians. I hope to hear more details of his stories, how he started the church, and how he maintained his courage, even when his fellow Christians didn't seem to. He suffered in prisons and gave his testimony before powerful rulers. Can you imagine listening to him tell about the time the Christ-haters stoned him and left him for dead? He'll tell us about the poison serpent that fastened itself on his hand. The people who witnessed that miracle expected Paul to die, but the snake had no effect on him, so the people mistakenly decided that he must be a god. Many times, the people looked on him and his fellow helpers as though they were gods, but Paul took no credit and revealed that all of the power of these miracles came from Jesus, whom they had crucified. I suppose Paul will tell of his shipwreck, the direction that God gave him, and how it all worked out just like God said it would. Paul was surely one of God's greatest disciples. Several books of the Bible were written by Paul as God moved him to write. Much teaching on earth was delivered by God through the Apostle Paul. We needed a man like him to start the church after Jesus went back to heaven. Paul will have a special place in heaven, and all will thank him repeatedly for his faithfulness and his example."

"Matthew, Mark, Luke, John, and Peter—how about them?" you ask. "And what about Timothy, Titus, Philemon, and James?"

"Oh, yes. Because we have studied the Bible and have heard these Bible stories, it seems as if we almost know these men personally. Can you imagine how much more there was to their lives? Only a small fraction was told. There will be so much more to learn. Some of these men seemed to be strong disciples, not wavering, not quick to speak, very stable and faithful. One man, Peter, was changeable. He denied Jesus. He took things into his own hands. Sometimes he didn't have the faith that he should have had, yet Jesus gave him a great work to do. We will love to talk with Peter, especially those of us who were kind of like him in temperament.

"Joseph and Mary, the earthly father and mother of Jesus, will have much to share with us. The story of Jesus's birth in the stable and his growing years will be so interesting to hear from their perspective. And we will enjoy hearing from John the Baptist, who prepared the way for Christ. He will explain his comments in the Bible to us. Nathanael, who Jesus saw under the fig tree, seems like a very exciting character. I'm sure we'll want to hear his story. Then there was Lazarus, Jesus's good friend who died, but Jesus awakened him. Don't you wonder what he'll have to say? We can ask Stephen about his zeal as well as his stoning. When he cried with a loud voice and said, 'Lord, lay not this sin to their charge,' we see his forgiving attitude. We'll meet Philip, Cornelius, Barnabas, Silas, and several holy women who helped in any way they could.

"There will be so many conversations in heaven. For example, consider the poor beggar at the rich man's gate. What a lowly fellow he was, but he became rich in the kingdom of God. Then think of the martyrs and many others down through the ages whom we've read about and whom we will meet in heaven. Our loved ones, too, will be there because they made the sacrifice to give up their 'self-life' in favor of a heavenly home above. The one common event that always happens to all who make it to heaven is the giving up of self, forsaking sinful desires and confessing sins, committing selves to Jesus, who humbled Himself to become our perfect sacrifice.

"If heaven seems like a faraway place, a long ways into the future, or a place you'll never enter, you must change your life," I finally say. "A true Christian life is a foretaste of heaven, and the true Christian has a vision of heaven in view. He sees beyond this world. His faith takes him in spirit to the 'land of endless day' the 'land of pure delight.'" The end.

Scripture References for Chapter 10

1. Revelation 7:17
2. Revelation 21:4
3. Revelation 21:25
4. Revelation 22:5
5. 1 Corinthians 15:52
6. Luke 16:26
7. Matthew 22:30
8. Luke 20:35
9. 1 Corinthians 13:12
10. Romans 8:17
11. Revelation 21:27
12. Revelation 10:1–6
13. Matthew 25:31
14. Mark 16:19
15. John 14:2
16. Hebrews 2:7–9
17. 1 Corinthians 2:9
18. Hebrews 1:13–14
19. Revelation 3:21
20. 1 John 4:7–21
21. Colossians 3:2
22. 1 Peter 2:11
23. Psalms 16:11
24. Mark 10:14–15
25. 1 Peter 1:18–23
26. Revelation 21:25
27. Revelation 20:10
28. Genesis 1, 2, 3
29. Genesis 6, 7, 8, 9
30. Genesis 12-26
31. Genesis 31-46
32. Exodus 2–40
33. Deuteronomy 34
34. 1 Samuel 19–31

35. 1 Kings 2
36. Psalms 1–110
37. Job 1–42
38. 1 Kings 17-19
39. 2 Kings 1-6
40. Judges 14, 15, 16
41. John 3:3–8
42. John 16:13
43. 1 Peter 1:18–20
44. Philippians 2:7–13
45. Acts 4:10–13
46. Acts 9:3–22
47. Acts 14:19
48. Acts 28:3–6
49. 2 Corinthians 11:23–30
50. Matthew 26:69–75
51. Matthew 1:21–5
52. Matthew 2, 3
53. John 1:45–51
54. John 11:1–45
55. Acts 7:59–60
56. Luke 16:20–2
57. Matthew 16:24–8
58. Hebrews 7:16
59. Revelation 22:1–5

How Is It?

How is it, that a man can be
Alive one day and able to breathe,
And the next day, his soul has fled.
He lies still, and cold, and dead?

It sure is cold, hard reality
To know one must spend eternity
Forever in bliss or terrible doom
After our souls rise out of the tomb.

We dare not take life for granted
Because of the seed that's been planted.
Sin will overrule and condemn us forever
Unless we repent, and self-life we sever.

Jesus has opened the door wide for you.

At the cross, a great light shone through.
The thief on the cross made his peace that day,
And wonderful words, he heard Jesus say.

Today, in paradise, you shall be with me!
Unspeakable joy and glory you'll see!
We'll walk by the river of that golden strand.
We'll listen and sing in heaven's wonderful band.

So live today like it's your last day on earth.
Humble yourself, accept Jesus's new birth.
Follow in obedience, have faith, walk the path
That leads to heaven and bypasses God's wrath.

Then tomorrow, if your breath ceases to be,
Nothing will matter until Jesus you see
Face-to-face, the redeemer of your soul
What a glorious sight while eternity rolles.

How is it that a man can be
Saved through all eternity?
Tears and pain and death all past,
Bliss and joy and love amassed!

   And

How is it that a man can be
Lost through all eternity?
Pain and torments and misery complete,
Never a chance the Savior to meet!

So

Now is the time to seek Him out.
Let Him tell you what it's all about.
The last day will reveal your fate at last.
Make it as sure as you can and fast.

—Bill Wesenberg

About the Author

I was born to a Christian family in 1956. I have 1 sister and 2 brothers. My wife and I have 2 girls and 2 boys. We are self employed. Our main business is truck farming. We also sell books and haul pontoons for a local company.